THE MACROECONOMIC MIX IN THE INDUSTRIALIZED WORLD

The high inflation coupled with high unemployment from which the world has suffered in recent years remains unresolved; for lower inflation appears to have been achieved only with high levels of unemployment.

In two earlier books – *The Macroeconomic Mix to Stop Stagflation* and *Unemployment, Inflation and New Macroeconomic Policy* – the author argued that the prevailing policies of rising tax rates, rising ratios to total output of the more inflationary forms of government outlays, and generally expansionary monetary policy, could have been expected to increase the upward pressure on the price level at any given level of unemployment; and that a correction of these policy errors was necessary in order to stop stagflation.

The present book argues that the evidence from the principal industrialized countries is consistent with the view that the setting of these macroeconomic instruments has been partly responsible for the world's macroeconomic problems.

J. O. N. Perkins is Professor of Economics at the University of Melbourne. He has also been a Research Fellow at the Australian National University, and has worked on the editorial staff of *The Economist*.

Among his previous publications are *Unemployment, Inflation and New Macroeconomic Policy*; *The Macroeconomic Mix to Stop Stagflation*; *The Australian Financial System since the Campbell Report*; *Contemporary Macroeconomics* (co-author); *Macroeconomic Policy in Australia*; *The Sterling Area, the Commonwealth and World Economic Growth*; *International Policy for the World Economy*; *Crisis-point in Australian Economic Policy?*; *Australia in the World Economy*; *Billion Dollar Questions*; *Macroeconomic Policy* (co-author and editor); *The Banks and the Capital Market* (co-author); *Britain and Australia*; and *Sterling and Regional Payments Systems*.

THE MACROECONOMIC MIX IN THE INDUSTRIALIZED WORLD

J. O. N. Perkins
Professor of Economics
University of Melbourne

With an Econometric Appendix
by Tran Van Hoa
Senior Research Fellow
Institute of Applied Economic and Social Research
University of Melbourne

MACMILLAN

First published 1985

Published by
THE MACMILLAN PRESS LTD
Houndmills, Basingstoke, Hampshire RG21 2XS
and London
Companies and representatives
throughout the world

Printed in Hong Kong

British Library Cataloguing in Publication Data
Perkins, J.O.N.
The macroeconomic mix in the industrialized world.
1. Macroeconomics 2. Organization for Economic Cooperation and Development Countries
—Economic Policy
I. Title
339'.0917'7 HC59
ISBN 0-333-38591-8

Contents

List of Tables

List of Charts

Preface

This book is intended to complement the *a priori* analysis of two earlier books, *The Macroeconomic Mix to Stop Stagflation* and *Unemployment, Inflation and New Macroeconomic Policy*, by considering some readily available evidence of the mix in the OECD countries since the later 1960s, and how the setting of the main macroeconomic instruments appears to have been related to relative success or failure in macroeconomic policy.

There is clearly a strong association between relatively high inflation at any given level of unemployment and a tendency for budgetary ratios to rise and monetary growth rates to be relatively high (and real interest rates relatively low). The evidence assembled here is thus consistent with the hypothesis being tested. But it is to be hoped that more sophisticated econometric methods will in future be widely used to test the mixes employed in various countries, and to compare them.

In the course of the preparation of this book the author has benefited greatly from discussions with colleagues and with economists in other countries. Special thanks are due to the following (none of whom bears any responsibility for remaining deficiencies), who have either read drafts of parts of the book or made stimulating and helpful suggestions in the course of discussions: Walter Eltis, Ian McDonald, Peter MacGregor, Kirker Stephens. A special word of thanks is due to my colleagues Duncan Ironmonger and Jimmy Tran Van Hoa for their work on testing the mix, much of which is embodied in the Appendix.

Helpful comments were received in the course of seminars at the Universities of Helsinki, Oklahoma and Stirling.

My thanks are also due to the London School of Economics for its hospitality during a substantial period while the book was being completed.

Melbourne J.O.N.P.

1 Introduction

The high rates of both unemployment and inflation that have prevailed virtually throughout the industrialised world in recent years, and the adverse effects that this has had, and is having, upon the rest of the world, presents the most serious economic situation since World War II. These problems remain scarcely less serious in the light of some degree of economic recovery in parts of the industrialised world; for the general level of unemployment has remained very high, and governments fear that if they introduce policies that succeed in greatly reducing unemployment this will make inflation rise sharply again. The policies employed in the industrialised world to handle this combination of unemployment and inflation have been manifestly unsuccessful in simultaneously reducing both inflation and unemployment to acceptably low levels, and there are few observers (if any) who appear able to suggest with confidence any consistent alternative policy that might reasonably be expected to succeed in that aim.

The present writer has put forward in two earlier books *a priori* arguments for believing that the sort of policies that have been applied in most of the OECD over the past decade are in fact those that might have been expected to bring about the sort of combination of high unemployment and high rates of inflation that have indeed resulted.* The present study complements the analysis and policy recommendations made in those books by examining statistical evidence about the macroeconomic performance and the macroeconomic policies of OECD countries to see whether it appears to support those *a priori* arguments; and to consider whether that evidence is consistent with the policy prescriptions given in the earlier studies, rather than supporting the (very different) combinations of policy measures that have generally been applied in most OECD countries over the past decade or so.

* *The Macroeconomic Mix to Stop Stagflation*, Macmillan, London, 1979; and *Unemployment, Inflation and New Macroeconomic Policy*, Macmillan, London, 1982.

The basic proposition of the present study is that most macroeconomic policy decisions, and most discussions of them, have in recent years apparently been taken against the background of a framework of thought that has too few dimensions. Discussion has usually been focused on such magnitudes as: the effect of policy decisions on the budget deficit (or the public sector borrowing requirement); or on particular monetary aggregates; or on likely changes in total demand (in 'nominal' terms). For most of the period up to the late 1960s an approach in terms of changing the general level of demand served fairly well: governments took steps to raise total demand (in nominal terms) when unemployment was too high and to reduce it when inflation was felt to be excessive. If they were concerned also about the balance of payments they often used a framework of thought that involved not only the choice of measures that affect total expenditure – monetary and budgetary policy (or 'expenditure-changing' instruments); but also instruments that influence the proportion of any given level of expenditure that is directed towards imports or exportable goods (compared with home-produced goods), such as a change in the exchange rate, or in some types of measures (such as a prices and incomes policy) that might directly reduce inflation (at a given level of employment) in the country relative to that in the rest of the world ('expenditure-switching' instruments, as they are often called).

But such a one-dimensional framework (or a framework of two dimensions in an open economy with generally fixed exchange rates) is not sufficient if a country has to concern itself with both inflation and unemployment at the same time. For policy has then to be directed not only towards changing the total level of spending (or influencing monetary aggregates or the budget deficit), but towards *finding the most appropriate combination of measures to change expenditure* (or to reduce the growth of the monetary aggregate in question), *in such a way as to minimise both inflation and unemployment.*

An analogy would be if one were given a one-dimensional instruction about how to find one's room in an unfamiliar hotel. If the manager points in the general direction of the room – but straight through a wall, rather than by directing one to go down a corridor and then to take the appropriate turning – such a one-dimensional instruction might serve in some circumstances, but would usually be hard to follow. This would be roughly the equivalent of the single instruction to increase demand when unemployment was too high and to reduce it when there was too much inflation. A two-dimensional plan of the hotel would be more useful; and, in the same way, a better framework within which to think about macroeconomic policy may well be to look not only at effects on aggregate demand, but also at the change in monetary aggregates that is occurring at the same time.

But even a two-dimensional plan would help one to find merely the right corner of the hotel, without ensuring that one would go to the floor on which the room was situated. In order to find both the right floor and the right corner of it, one would need a three-dimensional plan (or, of course, some other sort of instruction that covered also the vertical dimension – which usually takes the form of a hotel-room number of which the first digit in the number makes it clear on which floor it is situated). The macroeconomic analogy would be a framework of thought that asks not merely about the effects of policy on total demand, or only on demand and the quantity of money (or the budget deficit); but one that also tells the policy-maker to ensure that the combinations of tax rates, government outlays and monetary measures (principally sales of government bonds to the non-bank public) are such as to ensure that inflation and unemployment are both kept as low as possible. In order to achieve the appropriate combination of macroeconomic objectives the policy-maker needs to think in terms of at least two instruments even in a closed economy, when there is both inflation and unemployment; and normally in at least three if there is also some other objective – such as the state of the balance of payments ('external balance'), or the level of capital inflow, or the ratio of total investment to total output.

A two-dimensional road map of the Netherlands may well be all one needs to find the best route between two points in such terrain; but on a holiday in the Alps one would need a map with contour lines, or some other indication of altitudes, in order to find the best way between two places. It should not, therefore, be surprising that one needs a more detailed view of macroeconomic policy-making, with an additional dimension, to handle the problems of economies that can simultaneously suffer from both serious inflation and high levels of unemployment, whereas simpler models – with fewer dimensions – served reasonably well in the less complex macroeconomic situations of the 1950s and 1960s.

ARITHMETICAL EXAMPLE OF POLICY MIX

The basic propositions of this argument may be illustrated by considering the use of two alternative policies for reducing unemployment (say, by 1%) over some period, one of them being more inflationary than the other. Let us suppose that a tax cut is less inflationary (for a given effect on unemployment) than is a policy of monetary expansion. (The precise extent of the relative effects on inflation is immaterial to the general tenour of the argument, provided only that one instrument is – in the above sense – more inflationary than the other.) It will here be assumed that the proportionate effects of the two alternative policy instruments on each of these macroeconomic objectives remain the same over the range that is being discussed, and that their respective relative effects on the two basic macro-objectives remain if they are reversed. The basic argument would not, however, be affected, provided that the same instrument as before retains some degree of superiority in influencing inflation for a given effect on unemployment – even if the degree of its superiority is not the same when the instruments are moved in the reverse direction. If the degree of superiority were different when the instruments were moved in the reverse directions, appropriate alterations to the arithmetic would of course have to be made. Very simple figures have been selected in the following example.

It will be assumed in this example that any expansionary measure that reduces unemployment will make inflation worse over the period in question. This may not necessarily be true; but if it is not, the situation is much easier for the policy-maker, in that there would then be a single policy change that would reduce both inflation and unemployment, or at least reduce unemployment without making inflation worse. The example is thus addressed to pointing out that *even if* all measures that reduce unemployment made inflation worse over the period in question, there would still – on the stated assumptions – be a combination of measures that would reduce both inflation and unemployment.

It will be assumed that a tax cut increases inflation (over the year or other period for which policy is being considered) by 1% for each reduction (over the same period) of 1% in unemployment, and that a tightening of monetary policy reduces inflation by 2% for every increase of 1% in unemployment. This means that a tax cut sufficient to reduce unemployment by 3% will increase inflation by 3%, and a simultaneous tightening of monetary policy sufficient to *increase* unemployment by 2% will reduce inflation by 4%; so that the net effect of adopting both measures simultaneously will be to reduce unemployment by 1% (3% minus 2%) and also to reduce inflation by 1% (4% minus 3%). Provided that we have any two instruments with different relative effects on inflation and unemployment there is therefore no point in tolerating temporarily high unemployment merely in the hope that it will reduce the rise in the price level over the period in which the policy-maker is interested.

	Effect on unemployment	*Effect on inflation*
Tax cut	– 3%	+ 3%
Tightening of monetary policy	+ 2%	– 4%
Both the above together	– 1%	– 1%

By changing the signs in this example it can be easily seen that if tax increases had been used to try to check inflation and an easing of monetary policy to reduce unemployment, that would have made both inflation and unemployment worse.

THE POLICY MIX AND THE CURRENT ACCOUNT OF THE BALANCE OF PAYMENTS

Similarly, if there are two alternative measures that will reduce unemployment by 1%, and instrument A worsens the current account of the balance of payments by 1 million, whereas instrument B worsens it by 2 million, unemployment can be reduced, whilst simultaneously *improving* the balance of payments, by an appropriate expansion through instrument A and contraction through B.

For example, an expansion through instrument A (which might be tax cuts) sufficient to reduce unemployment by 3%, and so to worsen the current account by 3 million, accompanied by a contraction through instrument B (perhaps a tighter monetary policy) – which, taken alone, would increase unemployment by 2% and improve the balance of payments by 4 million – will thus reduce unemployment by 1% (3% minus 2%) and improve the current account by 1 million (4 minus 3 million).

If the exchange rate is free to vary (which is the appropriate assumption to make for most countries today, as being closer to the truth than the assumption of fixed exchange rates) this example should be interpreted as showing alternative effects of the two instruments on the exchange rate, rather than on the balance of payments.

	Effect on unemployment	*Effect on balance of payments*
Instrument A	− 3%	− 3 million
Instrument B	+ 2%	+ 4 million
Both together	− 1%	+ 1 million

A negative movement of the balance of payments could then be interpreted to mean a depreciation of the currency – say, by 3% at the top of the right-hand column in the above example; whereas a positive movement of the balance of payments should then be interpreted as a tendency for the exchange rate to be correspondingly stronger than it would otherwise have been – say, an appreciation of 4% in the middle line of the right-hand column. The general argument is, then, that provided that there are some ways of reducing unemployment that have less upward effect on the price level – or less effect on the balance of payments (or the exchange rate) – than some alternative way of reducing unemployment by the same amount, there is a combination of the two that will reduce both unemployment and inflation, or the balance of payments deficit, over the period under consideration. Obviously, if there were some measure that would simultaneously improve the situation on both fronts (by reducing both inflation and unemployment, or reducing unemployment and the balance of payments deficit) by itself, there would be no need to accompany that measure by some other. The above argument is thus directed towards the more difficult situation where all measures that reduce unemployment are assumed to have some upward effect on the price level, or, in an open economy, some tendency to make the balance of payments deteriorate or the exchange rate depreciate.

The next chapter outlines the *a priori* reasons why certain types of macroeconomic measures to reduce unemployment may be expected to have a greater upward effect on the price level than others. The three following chapters examine the experience of the industrialised countries that are members of the Organisation for Economic Co-operation and Development (the OECD) to see how far the available evidence is consistent with the view that rising tax rates, rising ratios of certain types of government outlays to total output, as measured by the Gross Domestic Product (the GDP), and relatively rapid monetary growth or low real interest rates, tend to increase the upward pressure on the price level at any given level of unemployment. Clearly, if expansionary monetary measures are more inflationary (for a given effect in reducing unemployment) than is a tax cut having the same effect on unemployment; or if increases in government outlays tend to raise the price level by more than a tax cut having the same effect on unemployment, the correct prescription for policy is to give as much of the stimulus as possible by tax cuts, and to restrain demand where necessary mainly by tightening monetary policy or restraining the more inflationary types of government outlays. If the countries that have had least inflation tended to have policies that come closer to this prescription than those of others; or if the groups of countries that had policies that conformed most closely to the above prescription also generally had more success in holding down inflation in a given period, then this would be consistent with the *a priori* arguments for adopting the mix in question. The basic reasons for believing that high or rising tax rates, high or rising ratios of some forms of government outlays to GDP, and rapid monetary growth or low real interest rates make it harder to restrain inflation are summarised in the next chapter.

2 The Basic Argument

The general hypotheses (argued in detail in the two earlier books referred to in the footnote on p. 1 against which the experience of the OECD countries is here being viewed, rest on the view that the particular combinations of monetary policy, taxation and government outlays that are chosen by a country (or by a group of countries) has an appreciable influence upon the extent of upward pressure on the price level that occurs at any given level of employment (or unemployment). In particular, the cost-increasing effects of high taxes, and also the price and cost-increasing effects of many types of government outlays, mean that (other things equal) a high, or at least a rising, level of taxation and of the more inflationary forms of government outlay, will tend to exert greater upward pressure on prices (at a given level of employment) than will a lower level of taxation and lower levels of those particular forms of government outlays. At the same time, there are other forms of government outlay – for example, on many types of capital works, including roads, and on many types of education – that may be able to do a good deal (at least in the medium or longer run) to hold down the rate of inflation by increasing productivity in one way or another; for example, better roads may bring goods to market at lower transport cost, and to that extent hold down the price level of the finished goods. For this reason, a prejudice against government outlays *as such* (on the invalid assumption that these outlays are *all* especially inflationary) is at least as misguided as a preference for trying to reduce unemployment simply by *increasing* (any or all) types of government outlay.

It is true that all forms of outlay that increase demand by a given amount in nominal terms – whether private consumption or investment, or government demand for goods and services – may be expected to have the same upward effect on the price level *if* they all also have the same effect on the available supplies of goods and services and the costs of producing those goods. But whereas many forms of stimulus – an easing of monetary policy, and increased expenditure by governments on goods and services, or on transfer payments, for example – add immediately to effective demand without directly adding to output, some forms of stimulus may simultaneously lead to an increase in the output of goods and services – for example, a tax cut that is directed towards subsidising extra output or employment by businesses, and perhaps a cut in any taxes that are paid by businesses. Subsidies on production may also lead to the subsidised goods being offered to the public at lower prices.

It may also often be true that cuts in taxes paid by wage and salary-earners will have some effect in restraining their wage and salary demands; so that wage and salary costs are held down to some extent by this form of stimulus. Moreover, some forms of tax give rise to a diversion of resources towards evasion and avoidance, which might otherwise have been used to increase productive efficiency; in particular, some of the most ingenious minds in the country may be consequently diverted to finding loopholes in the tax laws – and others to closing these loopholes up again. By diverting productive effort from producing goods and services sold on the market to these socially non-productive pursuits, the high tax rates may thus reduce productivity, and so raise the price level at any given level of employment or money incomes.

There may also be, on balance, adverse effects on the incentive to work, and to save, when tax rates reach high levels, though this is by no means certain, and the present writer would accordingly not place much weight on this consideration in the absence of clearer evidence about the direction of these effects. The view that they may be significant does, however, appear to have had a disproportionate influence upon the views of the Reagan Administration in the US in its early days. Inevitable disillusionment with the optimistic view that such effects might be important seems to have served to obscure the much more convincing argument for lower tax rates that are the basis of the present argument. So far as the Reagan approach was to reduce tax rates, therefore, the present writer would argue that it was doing the right thing for what were probably mainly the wrong reasons. (One other element of the Reagan approach – a reasonably tight monetary policy – is also consistent with the views being argued here; but the high level and rate of increase of certain types of government outlays in the US would certainly not conform to the *a priori* arguments being outlined here.)

At the same time, the argument of the earlier books is that a tight monetary policy – in the sense of a level of bond sales by the government to the non-bank public that tends to maintain high real post-tax returns to the lender (that is, returns after allowing for inflation as well as tax rates on the interest income being earned) will tend to hold down the upward pressure on the price level (at any given level of unemployment); so that the tendency for real post-tax interest rates to be kept down by policy action during the 1970s made it harder to reduce inflation.

This effect may operate partly through the relatively rapid rise in monetary aggregates to which governments resort in attempting to prevent the rise in nominal interest rates that naturally occurs when inflation increases. If people have become conditioned to believing that rapid monetary growth will cause more inflation, then that consequence will follow, whether or not it would have resulted apart from this expectation. But there may be other channels through which measures that hold down the real return to lenders tend to increase the upward pressure on the price level. In particular, asset holders may try to move out of financial assets into real assets (such as real estate and gold bars), the output of which cannot be readily increased in response to this change in preferences; so that this tends to raise not only the prices of those real assets towards which they try to move (as the general preference for these assets over financial assets increases) but tends also to reduce productivity in the economy as a whole and to increase the price level, as the real assets in question are (almost by definition, if they are widely regarded as good assets to hold, and good hedges against inflation) ones whose output cannot be expanded as readily as that of goods and services in general.

Furthermore, there are reasons to believe that many forms of government outlay – most obviously spending on defence, and outlays on transfer payments (such as social security benefits) – tend to raise the price level at any given level of employment (compared with the situation if such outlays had been lower). This is because such forms of outlay create disposable incomes without directly adding to the available supplies of goods and services for people to purchase with the incomes thereby created. In other words, if, instead, the same level of disposable incomes had been created in return for the production of goods and services that people wished to buy, the price level would have been lower. This certainly does not mean that all forms of government outlay tend to raise the price level, or that they do so to a greater extent than other types of outlay. Many forms of government capital investment – in good roads, and in many types of training, for example – may well do at least as much as any private investment to raise productivity (in either the shorter or longer run) and to that extent make it easier to hold down the price level (at least when these investments bear fruit). Just as there are socially useful and socially wasteful forms of private outlays, so the same may be said of government outlays. But, unfortunately, the forms of outlay that governments find it politically easiest to restrain are often forms of capital investment, whose contribution to increasing productivity may be as high as any that of any other form of outlay.

It is important, therefore, that any generalisation about the possible effects of government outlays based on the evidence of what occurred in the period under consideration should be strictly confined to discussing the types of outlay that were principally responsible for the increases in government outlays during the period in question. There is already some reason to believe that the commitment of governments to restrain their outlays has led them to cut back mainly the more productively useful forms of outlay, because of the political difficulties in the way of cutting back those – such as defence and social security transfers – that are most likely to raise the price level at any given level of total government outlays or at any given level of employment.

It should be emphasised that the above discussion does not prejudge the case for or against defence outlays or social security payments on more general grounds. Governments may believe them to be so necessary or desirable that they are willing to suffer the macroeconomic consequences of a relatively rapid growth of such outlays. But if these types of outlays tend to raise the price level faster than other types of spending, it is important that macroeconomic policy-makers should be aware of this. For the conclusion would then have to be that, if these outlays are to continue at a high level, the general level of real post-tax interest rates will have to be correspondingly higher, at any given level of employment, if inflation is to be held down. The real risk, however, is that governments will try to finance these high outlays either by rapid monetary growth or by high tax rates – both of which will add to the upward effect on the price level to a greater extent than if the same outlays were financed by borrowing from the non-bank public.

These arguments, and the policy prescriptions that follow from them, are in direct conflict with the broad lines of the policies that have generally been followed by OECD governments throughout most of the period under review, and they also contrast with the most widely espoused policy prescriptions that have been read and heard in most OECD countries in recent years. For governments have been constantly under pressure from financial writers and from much of the business world to hold down interest rates, either by adopting a more expansionary monetary policy, or by running a smaller budget deficit (which those observers seem usually to assume – not necessarily correctly – will tend to hold down interest rates at any given level of unemployment); and to give any stimulus to employment by easing monetary policy. The present writer would argue that such policy prescriptions are potentially dangerous; for most forms of more expansionary monetary policy, and many types of measures that would reduce budget deficits (or increase budget surpluses), will make the problem of stagflation *worse*. Indeed, it is more likely that interest rates (at least in nominal terms) will be brought down by a mix of measures that establishes a given level of employment with *less* expansionary monetary policies, and that unemployment can best be reduced by certain types of policies that may well have the incidental effect of *increasing* budget deficits (especially as normally measured and recorded); although other types of measures that would increase budget deficits – notably, many forms of government outlay – could be expected to make it harder to achieve the aims of macroeconomic policy.

It is obvious that the policies followed in recent years have – to say the least – not been successful in solving the problem of stagflation; even so far as they have reduced inflation they have (in most countries) left unemployment intolerably high. The search for solutions might therefore most reasonably begin by considering alternatives to those policies, on the basis of the hypothesis that the policy measures generally adopted over most of the past decade or so have been making the problem worse. Even so far as the policies appear to have reduced the rate of inflation, as measured by the rate of increase in the price indexes over the last year or two of the period under survey here, governments still seem to fear that expansionary measures sufficient to reduce unemployment appreciably will lead to a rise in inflation to undesirably high levels. (One might describe this, for simplicity, as a 'crude Phillips curve' approach to policy; for the statistical relationship summarised by Phillips in his famous curve was widely interpreted in earlier years as implying that governments had a choice between either high employment with high inflation, or lower levels of employment with less inflation.)

In the sense that governments are not willing to take the policy measures required to reduce unemployment, for fear of thereby increasing inflation, the problem of stagflation continues, even in those countries that have reduced inflation to what they may regard as a reasonable rate. It is, in any case, essential that governments (and all those who influence or advise them) should draw the correct lessons of the period since the later 1960s, so that future policy may be better able to hold down inflation, without being tempted to resort to permitting high unemployment in the (probably misguided) expectation that such a policy will solve the problem, and on the equally questionable assumption that there is no other way of solving it.

The principal purpose of the present study is therefore to examine the statistical evidence in order to assess whether the policies of the main OECD governments between the later 1960s and the early 1980s appear likely to have been exacerbating the problem. The main argument is that (at the very least) they have not been moving the OECD countries towards a solution of it; and that the sort of policies that have the best chance of success are in many basic essentials contrary to those that were adopted or widely advocated over the period in question. This is not to imply that these policies have alone been responsible for stagflation. For other factors – the industrialising of many Asian countries that have consequently become effective competitors for many European and North American industries; the rise in the world prices of oil during the 1970s; faster rises in wage rates (which may not necessarily have been entirely the result of a misguided macroeconomic mix); work force trends; social security benefits; changes in the pattern of demand and production – have all presumably increased the difficulty of maintaining a given level of employment without undue inflation in the more industrialised countries. Moreover, other policies of the OECD countries – in particular, the trend towards higher levels of protection and other forms of assistance to less economic industries, including agriculture in Europe, Japan and North America – have also intensified the problem of stagflation, by reducing the rate of increase in productivity and levels of real consumer welfare, and thus made it harder to hold down the price level at any given level of unemployment.

In emphasising the role that can be played by moving towards a more appropriate mix of budgetary and monetary measures, it is not intended to discount the possibility that some forms of prices and incomes policies may also be able to play a worthwhile role in tackling this problem; though it seems likely that a macroeconomic mix of the sort suggested here would facilitate the operation of any prices and incomes policy, and that some form of explicit 'wage-tax trade-off', combining features of the suggested mix with some features of certain prices and incomes policies, would probably have the best chance of success. Moreover, better resource allocation policies are also essential. The purpose of the present study is not to assess the relative role that may be played by macroeconomic policies (compared with alternative types of measures) in alleviating the problem of stagflation, but merely to assess whether the available evidence suggests that the general direction of the settings of the main instruments of macroeconomic policy in OECD countries has been making the problem worse; and so whether a reversal of the direction of principal elements in these macroeconomic policies could reasonably be expected to contribute towards solving the problem of stagflation.

It should, however, be emphasised that the policy prescriptions do not depend solely upon the argument that the setting of macroeconomic policy has for the past decade or more been itself making the problem worse. For example, even if the main cause of the problem is some increase in the efforts of employees to increase their money wage rates (so far as that may have occurred for reasons not associated with the setting of macroeconomic policy instruments), it would still be true that if a mix of macroeconomic measures were adopted that reduced the upward pressure on the price level, such a policy would help to alleviate the problem – even though it would obviously not reverse that particular cause of the trouble, and should not be permitted to divert attention from remedying the basic reasons for it. Provided only that there are some forms of macroeconomic stimulus that are less inflationary than some alternative measure (for a given effect on employment) there is a combination of those two instruments that will exert a downward effect on both inflation and unemployment. It may well be necessary or desirable to adopt other types of policy simultaneously to deal with other causes of the problem. But the basic argument that a correct macroeconomic mix can help, and an incorrect one will make matters worse, is valid, whether or not the initial cause of the problem has been that governments have been adopting an inappropriate mix.

The statistical analysis of this book is thus relevant primarily for the light it may throw on the relative effects of different macroeconomic instruments on the price level and the level of employment (respectively), and so on the correct combination of measures for minimising both inflation and unemployment. Provided that the evidence and the *a priori* arguments for that view are valid, the policy prescriptions would follow, *even if governments had not generally been moving the setting of their policy instruments in directions that made it harder to prevent stagflation*.

For example, those observers who believe that excessive wage claims have been a large part of the trouble can reasonably argue that we should try to correct this distortion; but there is no reason why they should not simultaneously agree that an appropriate macroeconomic mix will help to minimise the extent of stagflation that results from the excessive wage claims. Indeed, it is quite consistent with this approach to argue that one reason for the excessive wage claims has been the high level of taxes imposed on the wage-earners, and in certain periods (such as the early to mid-1970s) an excessively expansionary setting of monetary policy; so that a better mix might help to solve this problem also. But the case for the better mix does not depend on that view.

In any case, even if excessive wage claims are to some greater or smaller extent responsible for the problems of particular countries, it is not convincing to argue that they are the source of the whole problem; and it is far more convincing to argue that part of the high level of unemployment has been the result of governments trying to hold down inflation by permitting high unemployment; and the combination of a better mix with a more expansionary policy would certainly deal with that part of the problem. If other factors such as excessive real wage increases have also been contributing to the problem, this would mean that some of the unemployment could not then be eliminated simply by raising the level of real aggregate demand (even by a combination of instruments that would hold down inflation). But the use of a less inflationary mix (at the given level of unemployment) would still be able to minimise the extent of upward pressure on the price level at that given level of unemployment, whether or not the change in the mix had the effect of reducing the upward pressure of real wage rates.

CONCLUSIONS

One way of expressing the underlying argument of this book is to say that the 'monetarist' approach and the approach by way of aggregate demand (what might loosely be called a 'Keynesian' approach) each contains dangerous half-truths; so that the influence that each of these approaches had in recent decades may in practice have done at least as much harm as good.

For the monetarist approach, taken alone, leads governments to take steps to reduce the growth of various measures of the quantity of money in existence; and some of the measures they may use for this purpose may do at least as much to increase unemployment as to curb inflation.

On the other hand, the approach that leads governments to expand aggregate demand when unemployment is too high (often termed a 'Keynesian' approach) – which sometimes leads people to argue that this would not make inflation worse, simply because there is so much spare capacity, has very often led them to take measures that in fact make inflation worse even at very high levels of unemployment. Neither of these adverse consequences is a necessary implication of applying these approaches; for if either approach had been applied with a more apposite mix of measures, the adverse consequences need not have followed. Each of these approaches to macroeconomic policy is, however, silent on the crucial matter of how to choose the mix of taxation, government outlays and monetary measures that will do most to minimise both inflation and unemployment in the process of bringing about the rate of monetary growth (in the one case) or the effect on aggregate demand (in the other). Neither of these influential approaches can, therefore, escape some responsibility for the combination of social suffering that has followed from the choice of measures with which their approaches have been applied.

When governments found that certain types of expansionary measures – such as easier monetary policy or higher government spending – apparently made inflation worse (even if they also reduced unemployment), they unfortunately often became disillusioned with so-called 'Keynesian' policies *in general* (on the inadequate evidence of the types of expansionary policies that they had been employing) – whereas the application of basically similar policies in terms of aggregate demand, but implemented with a very different mix, could have been expected to have a more helpful effect in reducing inflation and unemployment.

Yet there is an important element of truth in both the 'monetarist' and the 'Keynesian' approaches, though each of them needs complementing by elements that are absent from both of them. The typical monetarist approach is right to emphasise the inflationary effect that may result from excessive rates of increase of monetary aggregates – even when unemployment is high; whilst the typical 'Keynesian' approach embodies the truth that there are ways of stimulating real aggregate demand that need not cause inflation when there are considerable unemployed resources.

But, unfortunately for the macroeconomic health of the world economy, policy-makers have failed to give proper consideration to the question of how to make the right choice of the combination of measures with which any given restraint is applied to the growth of monetary aggregates, or to the particular combination of measures selected to achieve any given rise in real aggregate demand. Yet the proper choice of measures to be used in order to bring about any particular change in some monetary aggregate or in the level of real aggregate demand can have a vital bearing on the outcome, in terms of what change in real output (or employment) and what rate of inflation will result from any given monetary restraint or from any given stimulus to the level of aggregate demand.

If, for example, a government aims to reduce the rate of growth of monetary aggregates mainly by raising tax rates, rather than by measures of monetary policy (essentially the sale of government bonds to the non-bank public) it is likely that it will have more effect than it would wish in the direction of making unemployment worse and less effect than it would wish in restraining inflation (at any given level of employment).

At the same time, if a government seeks to stimulate real demand mainly by an easy monetary policy and by trying to hold down interest rates, or mainly by increasing government spending, it could expect to have a greater upward effect on the price level – and correspondingly less downward effect on unemployment – than if it had sought to raise real aggregate demand to the same extent by way of tax cuts.

In short, it is essential that governments should give at least as much attention to the combination of taxation, government outlays and monetary policy with which they achieve any given change in a monetary aggregate or in the level of nominal aggregate demand as they give to considering the direction and extent of the effect they are trying to have on either of those aggregates.

One obstacle to such an approach, however, is that it is far simpler to discuss a policy measure in terms of whether it adds to aggregate demand, or to some monetary aggregate (or to the budget deficit or to the public sector borrowing requirement) than to appraise the particular combination of measures whereby that effect is achieved. For it is naturally harder to think in several dimensions than to think in one dimension; yet it is impossible to appraise any given policy in a situation of stagflation – even to the extent of assessing whether it will increase or reduce stagflation – unless due attention is paid also to the precise combination of measures whereby the effect on aggregate demand, or on monetary aggregates (or the budget deficit), is to be achieved. For some combinations of measures used to achieve any given effect on one of these aggregates will be likely to reduce the rate of inflation at any given level of unemployment (and in that sense reduce stagflation), whereas other combinations of measures having the same effect on the aggregate in question will make matters worse.

3 The OECD as a Whole

International comparisons of statistics are notoriously unreliable, for the accuracy of the data and the definitions used vary greatly from country to country. Work done at the OECD has, however, greatly increased the international comparability of some of the relevant statistics, notably those for unemployment, in the principal OECD countries.

The analysis of this and the next two chapters considers first the OECD as a whole; and then, in Chapter 4, the evidence for some broad subdivisions of the OECD; and finally, in Chapter 5, comparisons are made of the experience of the seven largest OECD countries. The main question to be considered is whether the general setting of macroeconomic policy instruments during the period from the end of the 1960s to the early 1980s was moving in directions that could, on the basis of the *a priori* analysis of the preceding chapter, have been expected to worsen stagflation by increasing the upward pressure on the price level, even at fairly high levels of unemployment; so that much of the deterioration of macroeconomic performance over that period might be attributed to the particular combinations of taxation, government outlays, and monetary measures that were adopted.

Comparisons are made (in Chapter 4) between the US – which is by far the largest OECD economy, constituting nearly two-fifths of the whole – and the seven major countries (including the US), considered as a group; and also with the group of smaller OECD countries. It seems appropriate to treat the United States economy individually in this sense, as it is so much larger than any of the other individual economies. The rationale for this approach is that events in the US contribute to such a large extent to events in the rest of the OECD that comparisons between the US and the other, much smaller, economies are inevitably somewhat prejudiced by the fact that what happens in any one small OECD country is greatly influenced by what happens in the US – whereas effects in the other direction are very much smaller, or even insignificant. Comparisons between the US and the rest of the OECD (as a whole) are more illuminating in this respect; for in this case one is comparing two groups of more nearly equal size (the rest of the major seven constituting in 1981 just under half of the OECD's output compared with two-fifths for the US, and about 15% for the group of smaller countries).

INDICATORS OF THE MIX

All the indicators used in the following chapters to depict the setting of the main macroeconomic instruments are to some greater or smaller extent affected by factors other than policy decisions; the budget deficit (or surplus) is perhaps the best-known example of one of these indicators (often employed also as 'targets') that is affected by the state of the economy, including many factors outside the control of policy-makers – as well as by decisions about tax rates and government outlays. For in times of recession revenue tends to fall and government outlays on unemployment payments tend to rise, so that the budget deficit deteriorates without there having been any change in policy in an expansionary direction; indeed, that situation is likely to call for more expansionary measures, so that if the government reacts to the larger deficit by tightening budgetary policy further it is likely to make the recession worse. The various ways of trying to allow for these cyclical factors – to derive a so-called 'structural' budget deficit or surplus – are all less than completely satisfactory; but any reasonable allowance for them is better than using the actual budget deficit as an indicator of whether policy is 'expansionary' or 'contractionary' – still less of whether it should be eased or tightened (which depends also on the whole economic situation).

In the same way, if we are using the ratios of government revenue or outlays to GDP as an indicator of the setting of tax rates or government outlays it would be preferable to be able to adjust those magnitudes for cyclical factors. Estimates on this basis are available for many of the industrialised countries for certain more recent years; but as these are not available throughout, or for all the countries for which data on an unadjusted basis are available, for the most part the cyclically unadjusted data are those employed in the following analysis. To that extent a rise or fall in the ratio of government current receipts to GDP is certainly not necessarily to be interpreted as a change of policy, still less as an indicator of the effect of government policy on the level of total demand. But if the aim is (as here) to discover whether – all else equal – a rising ratio of government receipts or outlays to GDP appears to be associated with an increased upward pressure on the price level, it is not essential to know whether the ratio is high as a result of the government making changes in nominal tax rates, or whether the ratio is changing because of factors outside the government's control. The use made of these ratios in what follows is generally for the purpose of indicating the mix of macroeconomic measures that is being employed – rather than attempting to assess the direction of the effect of budgetary decisions on the level of aggregate demand – for which cyclically adjusted data are much more appropriate. (Some brief reference is made, however, to certain available cyclically adjusted data in sections summarising the relationship between changes in budgetary policy and economic activity.)

In any event, the main comparison to be borne in mind in this analysis is between the widely prevailing use of very simple target variables – such as changes in monetary aggregates, or in the level of total demand (or in unemployment) as indicators of macroeconomic policy (on the one hand), and the use of the best available indicators of the setting of taxation, government outlays and monetary policy (on the other). The basic question underlying the analysis is whether – with a given rate of growth of some monetary aggregates – there is greater upward pressure on the price level, at any given level of unemployment, if the ratio of government outlays or current receipts to GDP is rising relatively sharply. If attention to these rough indicators of all the three main macroeconomic instruments seems likely to give better macroeconomic results than attention merely to monetary growth rates, or to the level of employment, or the budget deficit, it is obviously important to look at such indicators of the mix – rather than just at budget deficits or monetary growth rates – if a rational guide is to be found for macroeconomic policy in a situation where both unemployment and inflation are serious problems at the same time, or when there is a fear that reducing unemployment may lead to an intensification of inflation.

If the worsening of inflation and unemployment in the industrialised world has been in part due to rising tax rates and government outlays and a generally easy monetary policy, there should be some evidence of this in the indicators of the setting of these instruments in the statistics for the OECD countries, which constitute almost the whole of 'the industrialised world' (on the usual definition – which covers industrialised countries outside the communist block).

INDICATORS OF THE SETTING OF BUDGETARY INSTRUMENTS

The trend of the ratio of tax revenue, or total current government receipts (more than 90% of which consist of tax revenue), to total output (as measured by Gross Domestic Product) is a reasonable indicator of the extent to which governments have been raising the level of tax rates. It is not a perfect indicator, however, in that as tax rates rise avoidance (the legal form) and evasion (the illegal one) – 'avoision' for short – are thereby encouraged, so that the revenue actually raised may not go up as sharply as the increases in the (nominal) tax rates. As one of the undesirable effects of high tax rates is to attract enterprise and effort into the socially wasteful activity of tax avoidance and evasion, and as high tax rates may discourage effort in normal productive activities (and thereby reduce both measured output and revenue) or divert effort into productive activities where avoision is easier, the rise in this ratio may well understate the extent of the social loss resulting from tax increases and, as the process reduces productivity, this misallocation of resources makes it harder to prevent increases in the price level.

At the same time, the ratio of tax revenue to GDP may vary from year to year for reasons not associated with increases in (nominal) tax rates; for other influences may be increasing or reducing GDP, and changing its composition in ways that alter the ratio of revenue to GDP, even without any change having been made in tax rates. But such qualifications as these do not seem of importance when (as in the present chapter) the aim is to examine trends in the ratio of tax receipts (or, as an approximation to this, in the ratio of total government current receipts) to GDP.

The ratio of government outlays to GDP may similarly be influenced not only by policy decisions, but also by many factors outside government control that affect the level or rate of change of GDP or its composition. But, again, a progressive rise over a long period in the ratio of government outlays to GDP seems to be a fairly clear indicator of policy relating to government outlays, even though the precise change in that ratio from year to year will be influenced also by factors other than policy decisions; and, in any case, the effects on the price level do not depend on the reasons for the change.

But the composition of government outlays varies greatly from country to country and from time to time: and caution should be exercised in drawing policy conclusions from the apparent effects of increases in the ratio of government outlays to GDP in a certain period or country; for it is logical only to draw conclusions about the effects of the changes in *the particular forms of government outlays* that were occurring over the period in question. For example, in many of the OECD countries capital outlays by governments represented a fairly constant ratio to GDP (or one fluctuating about a fairly stable level) in the period from the late 1960s to the early 1980s, whereas the ratio of government outlays on transfer payments to GDP showed a marked upward trend. It is therefore not permissible to draw from this experience the policy conclusion that any and *all* types of government outlays should be restrained (if the adverse macroeconomic effects observed during the period under survey are to be avoided in future). Indeed, it may well be true that the sorts of government outlays – especially certain types of capital spending – that were most restrained during the period under survey, could better have been *increased*; whereas it may well have been the increases in defence outlays and certain types of transfer payments that accounted for most or all of any adverse consequences that may have resulted from the rising ratios of government outlays to GDP. It would clearly be irrational to curb further those forms of government outlays that had already been the most restrained, in order to avoid reducing the rate of growth of those other forms of outlay that may have been causing most of the adverse macroeconomic effects.

INDICATORS OF MONETARY POLICY

It is especially difficult to find satisfactory indicators of the setting of monetary policy in the overall macroeconomic mix. The rate of growth of certain monetary aggregates has been widely used as an indicator; but these magnitudes are affected not only by the use of monetary instruments properly so-called (the purchase and sale of government securities, and other measures – such as controls over the operations of financial intermediaries – that operate directly on the public's holdings of financial assets without directly operating on the income stream), but also by the extent to which government outlays or tax cuts (both of which affect the streams of disposable incomes) may be financed by the creation of money. An important part of the present analysis is to emphasise that the effects of policy on the price level and unemployment may vary greatly for a given increase in a monetary aggregate according to whether it is effected in association with changing tax rates, or by changing government outlays, or through the operations of instruments of monetary policy. It is, however, reasonable to use monetary aggregates as an indicator of monetary policy, *provided that budgetary policy is being held constant* (in some specified sense – such as maintaining the same ratio of government outlays and current receipts to GDP).

There is, however, the additional problem that, with changing financial systems – especially the de-regulation of banks and other intermediaries, and rapid financial innovation – the same rate of monetary growth (brought about in a given manner) in a given country may have widely varying effects at different times. Moreover, as the financial structures of different countries vary greatly among themselves at any given time, a given monetary growth rate for the aggregate of a group of countries (such as the OECD as a whole) may have a widely varying significance according to the way in which it is spread across different countries.

Some estimate of real interest rates – for example, a nominal rate such as the yield on long-term government bonds, adjusted for the rate of inflation in the same year – may also be used as an indicator of monetary policy; but, ideally, one would like to have an estimate of the *expected* rate of inflation, for which the *actual* rate of inflation in the current year is only an approximation. In any case, if the real interest rate rises this is not necessarily an indication that monetary policy has been made tighter (even with an unchanged setting of budgetary variables); for it may merely be the consequence of other factors having reduced the rate of inflation, or increased nominal interest rates, over the year in question.

ASSESSING THE EFFECTS OF THE MIX

The basic hypothesis is that a rise in the ratio of tax revenue, or of (at least some forms of) government outlays, to GDP tends to exert upward pressure on the price level with a given setting of monetary policy, and at any given level of employment; and that a reduction in one or both of those ratios, or a tightening of monetary policy, tends to restrain the rise in the price level (other things equal) over the ensuing period – which may be of one year or several years.

The question whether a rise in unemployment tends to reduce inflation (or to increase it) is not part of the basic hypothesis under discussion; for even if a rise in unemployment does tend to reduce the rise in the price level over a given period it is pointless to use it for this purpose if a change in the mix will have the same effect. Nevertheless, in order to seek evidence of whether a particular change in the mix tends to have a helpful effect in reducing the upward pressure on the price level, it may be necessary to see whether the change in mix was accompanied by a change in unemployment that might have been the influence reducing inflation in the period in question.

It is also desirable to compare the basic hypothesis about the mix with two other widely held views about factors that may affect the change in the price level. One of these is the view that reducing the budget deficit tends to hold down the rise in prices. The other is that reducing monetary growth – irrespective of whether or not this is done by monetary policy measures – will tend to reduce inflation. This 'monetarist' hypothesis contrasts with the one under discussion in the sense that the mix hypothesis emphasises that the effect on the price level will be influenced not only by monetary growth rates, but also by the combination of tax rates, government outlays and monetary policy measures with which a given monetary growth rate is achieved. In other words, there is nothing in the mix hypothesis that a monetarist need reject; for the mix hypothesis merely adds additional dimensions to monetarist thinking.

But the policy prescriptions that follow from accepting the mix hypothesis may differ greatly from what a monetarist would recommend; for the mix hypothesis would lead one to expect that a given reduction in a monetary aggregate achieved by a rise in tax rates would be likely to lead to a bigger fall in employment or to less downward pressure on the price level (for a given fall in employment), than would the same monetary restraint brought about by a sale of government bonds to the non-bank public, or by a reduction in the ratio of the more inflationary forms of government outlays to GDP; whereas a monetarist would (presumably) not consider that the means of achieving the reduction in the monetary growth rate would be important, and would probably expect any or all of these methods to have their main effect in reducing inflation rather than in reducing employment. If, however, one accepts the mix hypothesis one will wish to compare the relative effects on output (or employment) and the price level of securing a *given* change in monetary growth by each of a number of alternative combinations of policy instruments.

If the basic mix hypothesis outlined above is valid, one would expect to find that in years when inflation was relatively high (and when unemployment was stable or even rising), the ratio of tax receipts to GDP, or that of certain types of government outlays to GDP, would generally have been rising, or that the setting of monetary policy would have been relatively easy (or, of course, some combination of these three) over immediately preceding years.

The present chapter examines the changes in indicators of these policy instruments for the OECD as a whole over the period from the late 1960s to the early 1980s, and finds that the deterioration in macroeconomic performance in the OECD countries as a group occurred alongside changes in the setting of the macroeconomic policy instruments that were generally in directions that would (according to the *a priori* arguments) have tended to increase the upward pressure on the price level at any given level of employment ('making stagflation worse', for short).

But both the deterioration of macroeconomic performance and the movements of some or all of these indicators of the setting of policy might perhaps all have been brought about by other factors: and the deterioration in macroeconomic performance might itself have been making these indicators move in the directions in question; for example, faster inflation might increase the demand for money, and the quantity of money in existence might be mainly demand-determined, and some forms of tax revenue and some government outlays might tend to rise as a ratio of GDP when inflation was relatively high. Much therefore depends on the timing of the changes in these indicators of the setting of policy. It is therefore of special interest that the evidence suggests that the policy mix began to change in directions that could have been expected to increase the upward pressure on the price level (with given unemployment) in the later 1960s, just before the macroeconomic situation started to deteriorate, but well before such factors as the rapid monetary growth of the early 1970s or the oil price shock of 1973–74, occurred to worsen the situation.

Further evidence (to be considered in Chapter 4) relates to the experience of sub-divisions of the industrialised world. If the relative setting of the policy instruments in the various groups moved in ways that help to explain the relative macroeconomic success of those different groups of countries better than the level of unemployment, or monetary growth, or changes in their budget deficits, this would constitute evidence that policies based on holding up unemployment, or restraining monetary growth, or reducing the budget deficit, are less likely to improve macroeconomic performance than adherence to the principles of a sound macroeconomic mix. If macroeconomic performance deteriorated most in those groups of countries where the trend towards what is prima facie an unsound mix has been strongest, this would constitute much more convincing evidence than merely looking at the trends for the industrialised world as a whole; for it might have been true that the observed association between performance (on the one hand) and the setting of the instruments (on the other hand) for the OECD as a whole was the chance result of macroeconomic performance deteriorating most in certain subdivisions, whereas the setting of the instruments was moving in the observed direction mainly in *other* groups of countries.

It is also desirable to proceed at a further level of disaggregation by comparing the experience of individual countries. Unfortunately, for any given country there will always be many other influences upon unemployment and inflation in any given period that are apt to obscure the effects of the setting of the main macroeconomic instruments. In order to allow for these other factors, and to isolate only those elements of their common experience that relate to the setting of macroeconomic instruments, the experience of all the seven major OECD countries over the period is drawn on in the Appendix (p. 113) to assess the effects of changes in these instruments, by an econometric technique that compares the rise in the price level in a given year with the changes in the indicators of the setting of the main macro instruments during the preceding two-year period. An allowance is made for the distinctive characteristics of each of the individual countries (by the use of country dummies) in order to generalise from their individual year-to-year experience so as to draw conclusions about the association between the rise in the price level and changes in the setting of these policy instruments.

One way of testing the basic hypothesis is to see whether periods in which tax rates and government outlay ratios have been rising especially sharply, or when monetary growth has been especially rapid, have been followed by especially rapid rises in the price level –

without this being attributable to other obvious factors such as an expansion of the economy in question to near-full employment from appreciably less than full employment. This approach is applied to the major seven OECD countries in Chapter 5.

In the present chapter prime attention is given to the trends in indicators of changes in the policy mix over fairly long periods; but special attention is devoted to the later 1960s and early 1970s, when the principal alternative explanations of rising inflation in the 1970s (falls in productivity growth, faster monetary growth, rapid rises in money wage rates relative to productivity, the oil-price rises) had not yet occurred; whereas the changes in the setting of macroeconomic instruments in directions that could have been expected to worsen the upward pressure on the price level (at any given level of unemployment) had already begun. During the later 1970s and early 1980s, it is more difficult to sort out the effects of changes in the macroeconomic mix from many of these other factors; but the movement in the setting of the policy instruments is consistent with the basic hypothesis that the setting of these instruments was tending to make inflation worse at any given level of unemployment.

THE MACROECONOMIC MIX AND 'OPENNESS'

The evidence for the OECD as a whole has a special advantage for the present purpose (as compared with disaggregated data) in that for such a large unit the mix of macroeconomic measures must clearly be a relatively much more important determinant of the macroeconomic outcome, relative to influences originating outside the area, than can be true of the macroeconomic policy either of any individual country or of smaller groups of countries. Of course, even the whole OECD area is subject to important outside influences, of which the two oil price shocks were important examples. But any smaller economy is clearly much more likely to be strongly influenced in its macroeconomic performance by changes in its foreign trade and in other influences affecting its balance of payments, including capital flows. For this reason, the evidence for smaller sub-divisions of the OECD as to the effects of the macroeconomic mix on inflation and unemployment has to be interpreted in the light of the relatively large significance of factors external to the country or group of countries concerned; whereas for the whole OECD group taken together the setting of macroeconomic instruments is likely to have a significance somewhat more akin to that which it would have in a closed economy.

THE MIX AND THE LEVEL OF ACTIVITY

The indicators of the mix that are used in this analysis serve merely as rough indications of movements in the three basic macroeconomic instruments that may have been tending to increase the upward pressure on the price level *at any given level of activity or employment.* The level of activity may itself tend to affect the indicators in question; but the basic proposition being tested is thus that – whatever the reason for the change in the indicator in question – the upward pressure on the price level will (at that level of employment or economic activity) tend to be greater than if the rise in the ratio in question, or in the monetary aggregate in question, had been less.

It is, however, also of crucial importance that governments should adopt an overall setting of their whole macroeconomic policy that will lead to a high level of economic activity. The main purpose of having a mix of macroeconomic instruments that will minimise the upward effect on the price level at any given level of employment is to remove the temptation for governments to tolerate higher levels of unemployment than they would otherwise have chosen, in the hope that this will reduce inflation. So far as that is true of the approach of governments to macroeconomic policy, the greater the extent to which the mix is twisted in appropriate directions – towards lower tax rates, lower ratios of the more inflationary forms of government outlays to GDP, and lower monetary growth (or higher real post-tax interest rates), the more expansionary can and should be the *overall* setting of budgetary and monetary policy (taken together).

It is important, therefore, to complement the study of the setting of the main individual macroeconomic instruments by assessing whether the overall effect of all of them taken together was sufficiently expansionary to minimise the level of unemployment; or whether the setting of the macroeconomic policy of the governments was generally moving the economy further below full employment (or further above full employment if it had already been full).

Taking together the setting of the mix and the overall effect of macroeconomic policy, it is then possible to judge whether governments were using combinations of measures to reduce recession (or excess demand) and to do so by means of combinations of instruments that were likely to do least to increase inflation.

BUDGET DEFICITS AND POLICY

If a government tries to reduce the upward pressure on the price level by restraining the more inflationary forms of government outlay, it is imperative that it should (at least) offset the depressing effect that the spending cuts will have on activity by making tax cuts on a sufficient scale to reduce the level of unemployment. If, however, a government merely cuts its own spending 'in order to reduce the budget deficit' it will generally thereby make unemployment higher. Indeed, the lower are government outlays, the *greater* the budget deficit may need to be if tax cuts are to be employed to prevent a rise in unemployment; and that would be preferable to the alternative of monetary expansion, which is the most inflationary form of stimulus.

To advocate a reduction in a country's budget deficit is to imply that the outcome would be better at a lower budget deficit *irrespective of the means by which this was brought about*. Yet one may doubt that this is what is usually meant by those who advocate such policies. They usually mean that they would like a reduction in government outlays and stronger growth in the private sector. Yet a reduction in government outlays – alone – is likely to *reduce* the level of expenditure on the products of the private sector (at any level of activity short of full employment), by reducing sales of the private sector to the government sector and also to those that it employs, and so worsening market prospects of the private sector generally. Cutting government outlays without any offsetting tax cut will thus make unemployment worse and not assist the private sector. If the implication is that the deflationary effect would be avoided by simultaneously introducing a more expansionary monetary policy, the advocates of such a mix need to explain why they believe that this would be preferable to restoring the profitability of the private sector by adequate tax cuts; for the presumption is that an expansionary monetary policy would be a more inflationary measure than a tax cut for ensuring that private expenditure does not fall. Yet to advocate a reduction in the budget deficit is to imply that even a *constant* level of government outlays coupled with a tax *increase* would improve the situation, whereas at a time when the aim should be to avoid increasing unemployment, with as little inflation as possible, a tax increase coupled with a given level of government outlays will certainly make unemployment *higher* and *increase* cost-inflation.

In short, basing a policy prescription on what change should be made to the budget deficit or surplus makes no contribution whatever to illuminating the debate on macroeconomic policy issues. It is therefore a serious threat to rational discussion of the relevant policy issues that so many influential journalists, politicians and economists continue to use such phrases. The main purpose that such usages serve is to enable the user of them to avoid facing the real issue — which is the choice of a combination of monetary policy, government outlays and government receipts that is the most appropriate for stopping stagflation. Discussions of changes in the budget deficit therefore avoid spelling out the general directions in which each element in the mix should be changed. But unless the policy prescription is spelt out in at least the three dimensions of government outlays, government receipts and monetary policy, it can make no useful contribution to solving the problem of minimising both inflation and unemployment; for a government that adopts that prescription is likely to make the macroeconomic problem worse if it reduces the budget deficit by means of the wrong sort of mix of budgetary measures.

THE START OF STAGFLATION IN THE LATER 1960s

As Table 3.1 shows, during the years 1968–70 there was a clear rise in the annual rate of inflation in the industrialised world, to between 4–5½%, after it had averaged only 2½–3% between 1960 and 1967; and as this occurred without any tendency for unemployment to fall, this could not – on this evidence at any rate – be attributed to any tendency for the OECD economies to be operated at nearer to full employment. It therefore constituted a clear deterioration in macroeconomic performance. It occurred well before the decline in rates of productivity growth of the 1970s – real GDP per head for the OECD as a whole increasing at the same average rate between 1967 and 1969 as it had between 1960 and 1967. The onset of stagflation was thus also some five years before the first oil shock.

If the mix of the macroeconomic instruments was (at least in part) responsible, which of the available indicators of the setting of instruments showed a movement that would help to explain this deterioration?

Let us first consider whether a 'monetarist' explanation for the rise in inflation can reasonably be entertained. The series published by the IMF for monetary growth (on both the broader and narrower measures) in the industrialised world (a group of countries that is almost the same as the membership of the OECD) was actually

TABLE 3.1 *Macroeconomic performance and the macroeconomic mix in the OECD, 1966–82*

	1966	*1967*	*1968*	*1969*	*1970*	*1971*	*1972*	*1973*	*1974*	*1975*	*1976*	*1977*	*1978*	*1979*	*1980*	*1981*	*1982*
Rise in consumer price index (% per annum)	3.5	3.1	4.0	4.8	5.6	5.3	4.7	7.8	13.4	11.3	8.6	8.9	7.9	9.8	12.8	10.5	7.8
Rise in GDP implicit price index (% per annum)	3.7	3.1	4.1	4.8	5.8	6.1	5.6	7.7	11.7	10.9	8.1	8.1	8.3	9.6	12.0	10.7	7.3
Unemployment (% of labour force) (i)	2.3	2.8	2.8	2.6	3.1	3.6	3.7	3.3	3.5	5.2	5.3	5.3	5.2	5.1	5.8	6.7	8.2
(ii)	n.a.	3.0	3.0	2.9	3.3	3.8	3.9	3.6	3.9	5.5	5.6	5.5	5.4	5.4	6.1	7.0	
Current government receipts (% of GDP)	29.6	30.2	31.3	32.3	32.3	31.6	32.0	32.6	33.7	33.6	34.4	34.8	34.8	35.7	36.7	36.9	37.2
Change in year	+0.6	0.6	+1.1	+1.0	0.0	−0.7	+0.4	+0.6	+1.1	−0.1	+0.8	+0.4	0.0	+0.8	+1.0	+0.2	+0.3
Total government outlays (% of GDP)	30.6	32.0	32.3	32.2	32.7	33.3	33.5	33.3	35.3	38.4	37.9	37.8	38.2	38.6	40.2	40.9	42.5
Change in year	+0.7	+1.4	+0.3	−0.1	+0.5	+0.6	+0.2	−0.2	+2.0	+3.1	−0.5	−0.1	+0.4	+0.5	+1.6	+0.7	+1.6
Estimated real long-term interest rates (major seven) (%)																	
pre-tax	2	3	2	3	2	2	2	0	−4	−2	1	1	1	1	2	4	5
post-tax (40%)	0	1	0	0	−1	−1	0	−3	−7	−4	−3	−3	−2	−4	−5	−2	1

Monetary growth *(%)																	
OECD	n.a.	n.a.	n.a.	n.a.	n.a.	16.0	17.0	14.7	10.5	12.2	13.2	12.5	13.0	11.5	10.3	12.2	13.3
IMF (industrialised) countries)	8.9	8.9	10.6	8.1	7.4	13.9	14.4	14.7	12.5	10.6	11.6	10.9	11.7	11.4	9.6	9.2	10.3
Real GDP growth (%)	5.3	3.8	5.4	5.1	3.1	3.6	5.3	6.1	0.7	−0.3	4.8	3.8	4.0	3.1	1.2	2.0	−0.5

(i) Standardised basis, for the fifteen countries for which data are available.
(ii) Unadjusted data for all OECD countries.
*M1 plus quasi-money
'n.a.' signifies 'not available'

SOURCE OECD, *Historical Statistics*, various issues; IMF, *International Financial Statistics Yearbook*, 1983.

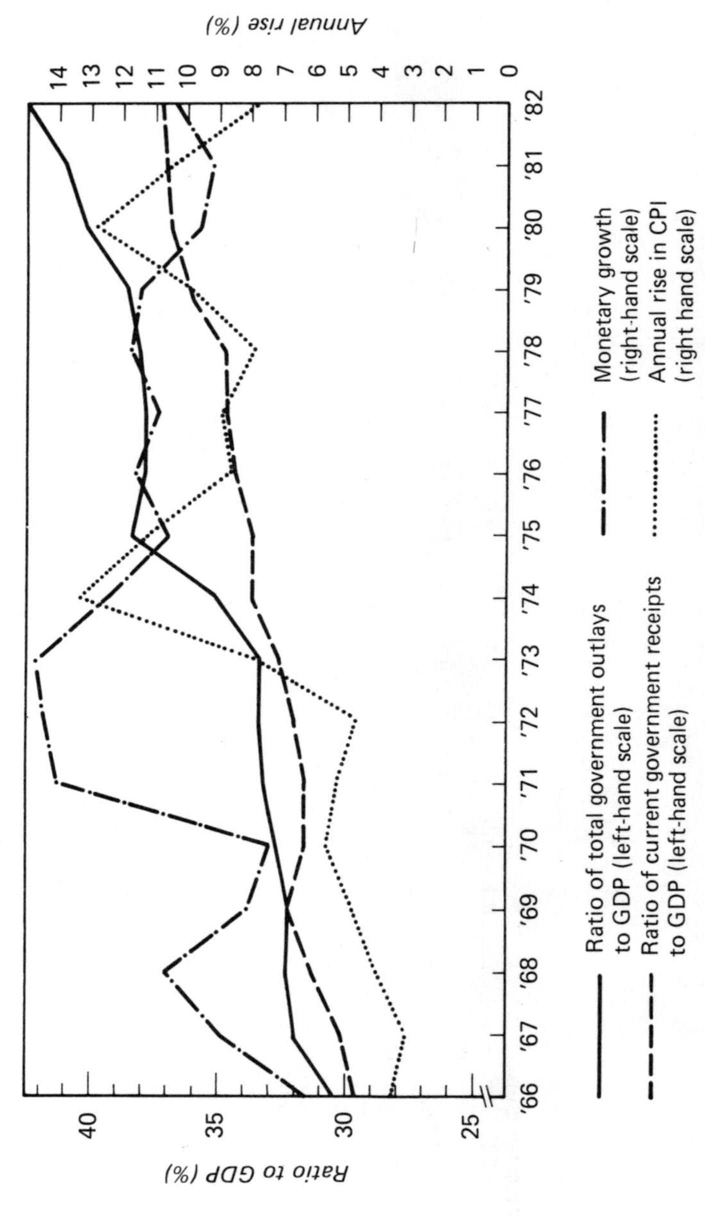

CHART 3.1 *Inflation and the policy mix, 1966–82*

slightly less over the average of 1966–69 than over the preceding four years (and real GDP growth averaged almost the same over these two periods). The increase in inflation in 1968–69 cannot (on this evidence) reasonably be attributed to any rise in monetary growth over the immediately preceding years.

Let us now consider the budgetary influences that the present analysis suggests may have been partly responsible for the onset of stagflation in the later 1960s.

Government current receipts had shown no marked upward trend as a ratio of GDP between 1960 and 1965, fluctuating within the range of 28.4 (in 1960) and 29.3% (in 1965). But a marked change occurred from 1966 onwards, as Table 3.1 shows, with this ratio rising by more than three percentage points within the four years 1966–69. The sharp rises in this ratio during 1966 and 1967 clearly preceded the sharp rise in inflation rates, which began in 1968, and the still greater increases in the ratio in 1968 and 1969 also pre-dated the further sharp rises in inflation in 1969 and 1970.

Government outlays, especially those on social security transfers, may also have played a part in the deterioration in macroeconomic performance at the end of the 1960s. For, after showing no clear upward trend as a ratio of GDP over the period 1960–65, total government outlays rose sharply in 1966–69 – especially in 1966 and 1967. This rise of 2.3 percentage points in the government outlay ratio during the years 1966–69 was, however, less than the rise in the ratio of government current receipts to GDP, which amounted to three percentage points over that period; but it nevertheless represented a marked change from the virtual stability of the government outlay ratio during the first half of the 1960s.

The increases in the budgetary variables in 1966 and 1967 happened before either the rise in inflation or that in unemployment had occurred. For these years at least, therefore, the situation is free of the complication that the association between higher inflation or higher unemployment (or both) and the rises in the budgetary ratios could possibly have been merely the result of higher inflation and unemployment raising these budgetary ratios.

It is also worth observing that this tendency for inflation to rise was not associated with a rise in the current budget deficits of the OECD as a whole; for (as we saw above) current receipts rose appreciably more than did current outlays over the period 1966–69. Clearly, therefore, so far as budgetary influences may have been important, it was the rise on either or both sides of the budget – rather than the change in the *difference* between them ('the budget deficit') – to which one should look for a possible cause of the problem. Indeed, for the average of the years 1968–75 the budgets of the OECD showed a surplus, in contrast to the small deficits shown over the period 1960–67.

The events of the later 1960s are thus consistent with the view that inflation can increase even when unemployment is also rising, and without any clear rise in monetary growth or fall in productivity, and with budgets moving in the direction of surplus, but after three years of rising tax rates and rising government outlays (especially on transfer payments, as Table 3.2 shows). Moreover, as these rising budget ratios occurred prior to the increase in inflation, they could not themselves be the consequence of that worsening of inflation.

1971–72

In 1971–72, the price level for the OECD as a whole rose rather more than on the average of 1968–70, but less than in 1970. It is difficult to attribute these changes in inflation rates to any concurrent or preceding changes in the rate of monetary growth. Monetary growth had slowed down in 1969–70 (when inflation rose), but then rose rapidly in 1971–72 (when inflation fell). Total current receipts of the OECD governments fell slightly as a ratio of GDP in 1971 (when inflation also fell), after several years of sharp increases, though the government outlay ratio continued to rise in 1971–72 at about the same rate as in the immediately preceding years. The rises in these ratios in the immediately preceding years thus appear more likely than the rate of monetary growth to have contributed to the worsening of inflation in those years.

1973–75

The years 1973–75 were dominated by the enormous rise (and subsequent fall) in oil prices, which is widely believed to have had the effect of increasing the general price level. But the very rapid monetary growth in the industrialised world in the years 1971 and 1972 was presumably an important reason why the oil price rise had so much upward effect on inflation. The oil price rise and rapid monetary growth were clearly two of the main influences increasing the price

TABLE 3.2 *Government outlays in the OECD (percentage of GDP)*

	1960	*1965*	*1966*	*1967*	*1968*	*1969*	*1970*	*1971*	*1972*	*1973*	*1974*	*1975*	*1976*	*1977*	*1978*	*1979*	*1980*	*1981*	*1982*
Total	28.3	29.9	30.6	32.0	32.3	32.2	32.8	33.3	33.5	33.3	35.2	38.4	37.9	37.8	38.2	38.7	40.3	40.9	42.5
of which:																			
current disbursements	25.3	26.2	26.9	28.3	28.7	28.4	29.2	29.6	30.0	29.8	31.6	34.6	34.5	34.4	34.5	35.1	36.6	37.3	39.2
of which:																			
final consumption expenditure	15.0	15.3	15.9	16.6	16.5	16.2	16.3	16.3	16.1	15.6	16.3	17.2	17.0	16.7	16.4	16.5	17.1	17.1	17.7
other current outlays	10.3	10.9	11.0	11.7	12.2	12.2	12.9	11.4	13.9	14.1	15.2	17.4	17.5	17.6	18.1	18.6	19.5	20.3	21.5
of which:																			
social security transfers	6.9	n.a.	n.a.	8.2	8.5	8.6	9.1	9.7	10.0	10.2	11.0	12.8	12.9	12.9	13.0	13.2	13.7	13.7	n.a.
capital outlays	3.0	3.7	3.7	3.9	3.6	3.8	3.6	5.6	3.5	3.5	3.6	3.8	3.4	3.4	3.7	3.6	3.7	3.6	3.3

n.a. signifies 'not available'

SOURCE OECD, *Historical Statistics: Economic Outlook.*

level in those years; but the ratio of both government outlays and current receipts to GDP continued to rise, so that the experience of these years, too, was consistent with the view that the budgetary ratios also had some upward effect on inflation.

1975–82

We have seen that inflation was rising even prior to the oil price shock of 1973–74, or the slowing down of productivity growth in the 1970s, and that experience of these countries from the later 1960s onwards was consistent with the view that rising tax rates, and also rising government outlays (at least in the form of social security transfers), played a part in worsening inflation from the late 1960s onwards, despite higher levels of unemployment. Moreover, from the early 1970s much faster monetary growth rates were also important.

But during the middle 1970s the aftermath of the first oil shock, and then the second oil shock in 1979–80, as well as the much slower rise of productivity (from the early 1970s onwards), clearly played a major role in increasing inflation. It may, however, reasonably be argued that without the much faster monetary growth rates from the early 1970s until fairly late in the decade, inflation would certainly not have been as bad as it was. The experience of these years is, however, also consistent with the view that the continued rise in the ratio of current government receipts, and of some forms of government outlays, to GDP also made inflation worse. Although government consumption expenditure did not show any clear rise as a ratio of GDP, and government capital outlays tended to fall (again, in relation to GDP), outlays on transfers rose sharply over the period (as Table 3.2 shows). In view of the rise in inflation in the period 1967–73, when oil prices and the subsequent fall in productivity growth had clearly not yet become appreciable influences on the macroeconomic outcome, but when higher tax ratios were already evident, it is reasonable to assume that the continued rise in government current receipts was also playing a part in worsening inflation during the later 1970s and early 1980s, and that rising outlays on social security transfers may also have been an important factor.

Those who believe budget deficits exert an upward effect on inflation, could, however, find support in the later years of the 1970s, when they averaged nearly 2% of GDP, in contrast to an average of only about 1% during late 1960s, and compared with virtual balance on the average over the preceding decade or so. It should, however be borne in mind that inflation was greatly reducing the real value of the national debt during the 1970s, and that this acted like a real budget surplus, whose effect tended to offset most or all of the effect on the real national debt of the nominal budget deficits that were occurring.

It is to be noted, moreover, that the rise in the budget deficits was not due to any cut in tax receipts relative to GDP, but to the rise in government outlays. This experience of rising budget deficits is therefore equally consistent with the view that it was the rising government outlays (and tax rates) that worsened the inflation, rather than the budget deficits as such.

Monetary growth rates in the 1970s were clearly much higher than in the early 1960s, and this factor could certainly be interpreted as helping to explain the much higher inflation in the decade or so from 1971 onwards.

The events of these years are clearly consistent with the view that the sharp rise in the ratio of government outlays to GDP played a role in keeping up the rate of inflation, despite the steadily rising level of unemployment.

It is difficult to cite monetary growth factors to explain the renewed rise in inflation in 1979–81. Certainly, the second oil price shock played a part; but there was no immediately preceding upsurge in monetary growth comparable to that which preceded the inflation following the earlier oil price rise.

1967–82 AS A WHOLE

In short, the experience of the OECD as a whole over the period from the late 1960s to the early 1980s is fully consistent with the view that not only high monetary growth, but also high and rising ratios of government outlays (or at least of government transfer payments) and of government current receipts to GDP helped to explain why there were high rates of inflation, despite the high and rising levels of unemployment. Clearly, other factors – especially the oil price rises and the slower productivity growth – helped to worsen the inflation. But the experience of the later 1960s and early 1970s, before oil prices and slower productivity growth became important, provides good evidence that rising tax rates (in the later 1960s) and higher monetary growth rates (from the early 1970s) were important. All these factors appear to have been significant at various times, and no one of them can reasonably be relied upon to explain more than part of the worsening macroeconomic performance.

BUDGETARY POLICY AND ACTIVITY

We have seen in the foregoing discussion that, virtually throughout the period from the later 1960s to the early 1980s, the main indicators of budgetary policy were moving in directions that could have been expected to make inflation worse at any given level of employment. We have also seen that for the OECD as a whole, the tendency of the net budget outturn in the first half of the 1970s (by comparison with the 1960s) was in the direction of surplus (or reduced deficits). There is no available estimate of what this implied in terms of changes in the stance of budgetary policy over the whole period and for the whole of the OECD; but over the period between the mid-1960s and the early 1970s unemployment was tending to rise, so that any reasonable cyclical adjustment of the budget outturn to allow for this would have indicated a still *larger* move in the direction of surplus than in the crude figures (as tax receipts were held down by the rise in unemployment, whereas government outlays were increased by it). In terms of its implications for the level of activity, therefore, one can conclude that the overall budgetary setting of the OECD countries was tending to force their economies somewhat further below full employment over that period even though other influences, too, were operating in the same direction, so that the appropriate policy prescription ought to have been to use the budget so as to have an expansionary effect. But the very high monetary growth rates were in fact generating inflationary pressure – and in the process were making governments increasingly (though unjustifiably) disillusioned with trying to use macroeconomic policy to maintain full employment. The conclusion that they should have drawn, however, was *not* that *all* forms of macroeconomic expansion are liable to be inflationary (and perhaps not even successful), but that if they rely on monetary expansion (especially if it leads to low or negative real post-tax interest rates) they can expect high rates of inflation to result.

From 1973 onwards we have some estimates of cyclically adjusted budgets for a number of major countries, which will be referred to in Chapters 4 and 5. For the OECD as a whole, however, it can be judged from OECD estimates (based on figures for the major seven and ten other countries), shown in Table 3.3 that the tendency for nominal budget deficits to increase in the later 1970s was largely a result of tax receipts being held down as a result of rising unemployment and of increasing government outlays on unemployment benefit payments. To judge from the OECD estimates of cyclical adjustments for almost all the OECD countries for 1978–82, especially the bottom line of Table 3.3 (which is derived from them) the rise in nominal budget deficits in later years of the period up to 1981 thus represented *not* a more expansionary setting of budgetary policy but the effects of economic recession on the budgets.

Moreover, the high rates of inflation were reducing the real value of the national debt of OECD countries over this period, especially in relation to GDP. The consequent fall in the real value of the public's holdings of government bonds (discussed in Chapter 5) acted as a depressing influence on the expenditure of the public – as they sought to rebuild the real value of their diminished financial assets. The 'real' movement of budgets in the direction of surplus – after this inflation adjustment – was thus considerable.

In addition to the changes in the macroeconomic mix discussed in earlier sections, which were, as we have seen, tending to increase the upward pressure on the price level at any given level of unemployment, the overall setting of budgetary policy was thus making a considerable contribution over most of the period to increasing the level of unemployment.

The macroeconomic policies of this period should therefore be criticised on two scores: first, that they used a combination of measures that worsened the upward pressure on the price level at each level of unemployment; and, secondly, that the effect of changes in the general setting of budgetary policy was in the direction of raising the level of unemployment. These two basic errors of policy were inter-related, in the sense that when governments became alarmed at the high rates of inflation in the first half of the 1970s – which were partly due to the misguided mix of macroeconomic measures – they reacted by tolerating increasing unemployment, in the hope that this would reduce inflation. Yet they did this to an excessive extent by raising tax rates instead of by reducing the more inflationary forms of government outlays or by tightening monetary policy – at any rate up until very near the end of the period. Unfortunately, when they eventually decided to tighten monetary policy they failed to take

TABLE 3.3 *Actual and cyclically adjusted current government receipts and expenditures for seventeen OECD countries, 1978–82 (% of GDP)*

	1978	*1979*	*1980*	*1981*	*1982**
Total current receipts					
Actual	34.6	35.0	35.9	36.8	37.0
Cyclically adjusted	34.6	34.9	35.8	36.8	36.7
Change over year					
Actual	n.a.	0.4	0.9	0.9	0.2
Cyclically adjusted	n.a.	0.3	0.9	1.0	–0.1
Total government expenditure					
Actual	36.8	36.8	38.4	39.5	41.2
Cyclically adjusted	36.0	36.2	37.0	37.4	37.5
Change					
Actual	n.a.	0.0	1.6	1.1	1.7
Cyclically adjusted	n.a.	0.2	0.8	0.4	0.1
'Budget deficit' (expenditure less receipts)					
Actual	2.2	1.8	2.5	2.7	4.2
Cyclically adjusted	1.4	1.3	1.2	0.6	0.8
Change					
Actual	n.a.	–0.4	+0.7	+0.2	+1.5
Cyclically adjusted	n.a.	–0.1	–0.1	–0.6	+0.2

*OECD estimates and forecasts.
n.a. signifies 'not available'.
A negative sign before figures in the bottom line, for changes in the cyclically adjusted budget deficit, indicate a movement of the budget in a *contractionary* direction.

SOURCE OECD *Economic Outlook*, Dec. 1983, table 11.

sufficiently expansionary action by way of tax cuts to prevent this from increasing unemployment; so that the overall effect of their policies continued to be such as to hold down activity (until late in 1982), even though the mix of measures was not now so inflationary as it had been for most of the previous decade.

It was only at the very end of the period that a more expansionary budget, including tax cuts, in the US led the way towards a combination of measures that could generate recovery without giving an unwanted stimulus to inflation.

CONCLUSION

For most of the 1970s, therefore, a sort of vicious circle of deflationary changes in the setting of budgets and misguided changes in the mix characterised the macroeconomic policies of OECD governments. For the inflationary changes in the mix in the early 1970s – rapid monetary growth and low or negative real interest rates coupled with rising budgetary ratios – led governments to try to check the consequent inflation by permitting rising unemployment, for which governments were partly responsible because of the deflationary overall setting of monetary and budgetary policies. But just as the inflationary mixes in the early 1970s had led governments to the (wrong) conclusion that they could not safely act to reduce unemployment because policies aimed at doing so would (as they thought) worsen inflation, so the use of high and rising tax rates as a major element restraining demand in the later 1970s led to more upward pressure on costs than a less inflationary mix would have produced (for the same effect on unemployment), and to a greater downward effect on employment than would have resulted from a less cost–inflationary form of restraint.

Moreover, when governments reduced monetary growth, the fact that they did this to a considerable extent by way of high and rising tax rates led many observers to criticise 'monetary restraint' as a means of trying to curb inflation – whereas the means whereby monetary growth had been curbed was not merely, or not mainly, the use of monetary measures, but the use of high and rising tax rates.

In short, the use of inflationary types of mixes gave *expansionary* measures a bad name in the earlier years of the 1970s; and the use of inflationary mixes aimed at *restraining* demand in much of the later years of the 1970s (and early 1980s) also gave a quite unjustified bad name to anti-inflationary 'monetary policy' (which had *not* in fact really been the main form of restraint applied) over most of this period. If, instead, the expansionary measures used earlier in the decade had taken the form mainly of tax cuts, and much less the form of monetary ease and rising government outlays, governments would not have become so disillusioned about the possibility of providing non-inflationary forms of stimulus. Similarly, if they had placed most emphasis on monetary measures to reduce inflation – coupled with tax cuts as the main form of stimulus – unemployment need not have risen so far in the process of reducing inflation in the later 1970s and early 1980s.

4 Major Sub-Divisions of the OECD

In the previous chapter we saw that the general trend towards both higher unemployment and (at least until the very end of the period) generally also towards higher inflation was occurring alongside a tendency for the setting of the macroeconomic instruments to move in directions that could, according to the *a priori* arguments summarised in Chapter 2, have been expected to make inflation worse at any given level of unemployment.

For more convincing evidence of this association we now consider certain sub-divisions of the OECD, to see whether the groups of countries with the greatest deterioration of their macroeconomic performance tended also to be those where the policy indicators in question (higher tax and government outlay ratios, and high monetary growth) tended also to move most markedly in the directions that were likely to make stagflation worse.

The present chapter therefore considers the evidence provided by aggregate data published by the OECD for a number of sub-groups of OECD countries (many of them overlapping with one another). The use of such aggregate data acts as a simple averaging process, which thus tends to discount in a rough way for the peculiar circumstances of the individual countries in each group, so as to derive conclusions about those influences that they shared in common. It is important to do this in some way, for each country's macroeconomic performance is naturally influenced by many considerations in addition to the setting of the macroeconomic mix. For example, factors originating outside the country cause changes in its terms of trade and capital inflows and outflows, and such influences may well often be much more important, especially for small, open economies, than the setting of macroeconomic policy instruments in determining the rate of inflation and the level of unemployment in that country.

Moreover, countries may also vary greatly in their ability to tolerate high or rising tax rates or government outlays without adverse effects on their macroeconomic performance. For example, if the tax system is widely accepted as being equitable, tax increases may be much more readily accepted without their giving rise to higher wage demands than if the tax rise is perceived as being disproportionately borne by wage and salary-earners. Again, there may in some countries be a well established prices and incomes policy that enables the inflationary effects of rising budget ratios to be withstood without so much upward pressure on wages and prices as might result in some other countries without such a prices and incomes policy. Ideally, more sophisticated methods are desirable to abstract from those factors that are peculiar to individual countries, in order to draw conclusions from their common experience about the apparent effects of their mix of macroeconomic policy measures; and such an approach is applied in Chapter 5 to the experience of the seven largest OECD countries, in order to generalise about the apparent relationship to inflation of changes in the setting of macroeconomic policy instruments of the countries in this group over the period.

But it is also worth seeing what can be learned from the simpler approach of examining the indicators of the setting of macroeconomic policy instruments in groups of countries – the process of averaging by aggregation being a crude method of discounting to some extent to allow for the factors peculiar to individual countries.

The sub-divisions of the OECD for which the aggregate data are available include the major seven (the US, Japan, Germany, France, Britain, Italy and Canada) as a group, and the remaining OECD countries (the 'small-country' group). The US will also be considered by itself – being by far the largest country in the OECD; and its experience can be compared with the aggregate for 'the OECD less the US'.

In addition to these two sets of mutually exclusive groupings (one of them being the major seven and the small-country group; and the other set being the US and 'the OECD less the US' group), there are three other (to some extent intersecting) groups for which the relevant aggregate data are available from OECD published sources. These are the European Economic Community, OECD Europe (which includes the EEC), and also the aggregate for all OECD countries.

INFLATION AND THE MIX IN SOME SUB-DIVISIONS OF THE OECD

Table 4.1 shows the rates of inflation in the later 1960s and up to 1970, and also over the period 1971–81, for the various sub-divisions of the OECD by groups of countries for which data are available in this form, plus the data for the US alone.

For almost all of the 1971–81 period – though not for a brief period in the late 1960s to be considered below – the group of smaller countries had a higher rate of inflation than any of the other sub-divisions of the OECD. The grouping with the second highest rate of inflation (taking the whole period from the later 1960s to the early 1980s) was OECD Europe, followed by the OECD less US. The EEC was the median case, followed by the aggregate for the whole of the OECD, then the major seven, with the US as the least inflationary of these sub-divisions.

Before asking what part the macroeconomic mix appears to have played in helping to explain the relative success of these groups in holding down inflation, it is appropriate first to ask whether a more rapidly rising level of unemployment may have helped to explain the relative success or failure of different sub-divisions of the OECD in holding down inflation. For if relatively high or rising unemployment characterised those groupings that had most success in holding down inflation, that would provide some sort of prima facie support for the widespread assumption that high or rising unemployment tends to reduce inflation, and so for the policies that appear to be based on that assumption.

Table 4.1 therefore also shows the rise in the recorded unemployment rates for these sub-divisions of the OECD. It may be observed that there is certainly no obvious positive correlation between the degree of success of a sub-division in holding down inflation and the extent to which governments in that group of countries were apparently willing to let unemployment rise from its level of the later 1960s up to the early 1980s. In particular, the group of smaller countries experienced the highest rate of inflation over the period as a whole, yet this was also the group that suffered the *greatest* rise in recorded unemployment up to 1981 (and were still among the highest up to 1982); and OECD Europe had the second largest rise in unemployment up to 1981 (and one of the largest up to 1982), but also the second *highest* rate of inflation.

TABLE 4.1 *Inflation and unemployment, 1968–81: selected sub-divisions of the OECD*

	Consumer price index: annual percentage change					*Unemployment as percentage of labour force*		
	1967	*1968*	*1969*	*1970*	*1971–81 Average*	*Rise in unemployed 1968–81*	*Annual average 1968–73*	*1974–81*
Smaller countries	5.5	3.8	3.6	5.3	11.8	5.2	4.2	6.9
OECD Europe	3.3	3.7	4.0	5.1	10.6	5.1	3.4	5.9
OECD less US	3.4	3.9	4.2	5.4	10.0	4.1	2.9	5.0
EEC	2.7	3.6	4.2	4.9	9.7	4.6	2.7	5.0
All OECD	3.1	4.0	4.8	5.6	9.2	4.0	3.4	5.5
Major seven	2.7	4.1	5.0	5.7	8.7	3.6	3.2	5.2
US	2.8	4.2	5.4	4.3	8.1	4.1	4.6	6.8

SOURCE OECD *Historical Statistics*, 1960–81.

Similarly, it may be worth noting also that if we take the percentage levels of registered unemployment over the period 1974–81, the two groups with the *highest* rate of inflation had two of the three *highest* levels of unemployment (though this particular index of macroeconomic success is probably not worth emphasising, as the absolute level of recorded unemployment varies greatly with factors peculiar to the individual countries that may have little or nothing to do with macroeconomic policy).

If there is an association between these two indicators of macroeconomic failure – high inflation and rising unemployment – it could reasonably be argued that these figures suggest that it appears to be in the form of a tendency for unemployment to increase to a relatively *large* extent (and also for recorded unemployment to be relatively *high*) in those sub-divisions with the *highest* inflation – which is of course the very opposite to the relationship that one would require the evidence to show if it were to support a case for tolerating high or increasing levels of unemployment on the grounds that such a policy was necessary in order to hold down inflation.

If, however, one wishes to argue that the high rates of inflation occurred *despite* a tendency for rising unemployment to restrain inflation in those sub-divisions of the OECD that suffered the highest rates of inflation, this means that one is in the position of having to assign correspondingly greater weight to other factors – which would include the policy mix – to explain why inflation was relatively high in those groups that generally had above-average increases in unemployment.

MONETARY GROWTH AND RELATIVE RATES OF INFLATION

One element in the mix hypothesis is that relatively rapid rates of monetary growth, in relation to the rise in real output, tend to make inflation worse – with a given setting of the instruments of budgetary policy and a given rate of unemployment. But it is appropriate first to consider whether the simpler ('monetarist') view that monetary growth alone is sufficient to explain relative inflation rates (without introducing also considerations relating to tax rates and government outlays).

The emphasis on the relationship between monetary growth and inflation that is characteristic of monetarism need not, however, necessarily be thought of as distinctive of that approach alone. It is true that monetarists emphasise factors on the *supply* side that determine the quantity of money in existence. But the rate of growth of the *demand* for money also affects the measured monetary aggregates; and some would argue that those influences are the dominant ones. So far as that is true, any factor that increases the demand for money (including the cost-increasing effects of high tax rates) will tend to increase the actual stock of money in existence.

Such influences may operate through the greater readiness of bank customers to overdraw their accounts (an important consideration in countries such as Britain and Australia, where the overdraft method of lending is general), or through banks being readier to lend in response to a rise in the demand for money. It may also, however, be a result of governments relaxing monetary policy in the face of a rising demand for money, in order to avoid interest rate increases; but such government reactions are, of course, fully consistent with monetarist explanations, as they are a factor on the supply side.

If, therefore, we observe an association between monetary growth rates and inflation, this need not necessarily be evidence in support of monetarist views; for it may be that the association in question springs mainly from the reaction of governments to higher rates of inflation or from factors on the demand side that also affect monetary aggregates; and among those factors on the demand side may well be price-increasing effects of high tax rates and high levels of certain forms of government outlay. In comparing a 'mix' explanation of inflation with a 'monetarist' one, it is not intended to suggest that only monetarists emphasise the association of monetary growth rates with inflation. Indeed, the mix hypothesis is consistent with either of these approaches to explaining the association between monetary growth and inflation, without attributing that association either mainly to the supply side of the creation of money or mainly to influences on the demand side.

In any case, it is important not to use the phrase 'money supply' to describe the quantity of money actually in existence; for that aggregate is the product of both demand and supply factors, and to describe it as 'the money supply' implicitly pre-judges the relative importance of factors on the supply side. The analysis in the present book is consistent with widely varying views on this matter.

MONETARY GROWTH AND INFLATION IN MAJOR SUB-DIVISIONS OF THE OECD

As Table 4.2 shows, there has clearly been some tendency for the higher rates of inflation to occur in the groups of countries with relatively rapid monetary growth rates over the period for which the OECD has published the relevant data (from 1972 onwards for the broader of the two definitions of money that it publishes, that which it terms 'M1 plus quasi-money').

The top four sub-divisions on the criterion of monetary growth are also the top four in terms of rates of inflation. This is true whether one looks at the actual monetary growth rates over the period or adjusts them (as in the right-hand column of Table 4.2), to allow for the differences in the growth of real GDP in each sub-division. But *within* each of the two categories (that is to say, the four sub-divisions with both the highest inflation rates and also the highest monetary growth, as contrasted with the bottom three, which had both lower inflation and lower monetary growth rates than any countries in the top part of the table), the ranking of each sub-division of the OECD within the category in question is clearly different for relative inflation from what it is for monetary growth. The reasonable conclusion would be that relative monetary growth rates appear to have played some part in determining relative rates of inflation; or, if one prefers a non-monetarist explanation for this, that in groups of countries where other factors were making for high inflation, monetary aggregates tended to rise especially rapidly in response to the consequently rapidly rising demand for money; but that other influences were clearly also important in determining relative inflation rates.

In particular, monetary growth (adjusted for the growth of real GDP) for the sub-division with the highest rate of inflation – the small-country group – was, over the average of years 1972–82 (the whole of the period for which the data for 'M1 plus quasi-money' are available from the OECD for all the sub-divisions in question) less than it was for the OECD less the US, or for OECD Europe, or for the EEC – whereas the small-country sub-division had an appreciably higher rate of inflation than any of the other groups. Moreover, the EEC, with the fastest monetary growth rate relative to the rate of growth of real GDP (though it was only marginally greater than that for OECD Europe), was not among the top three sub-divisions in terms of rates of inflation. On the measure of M1 alone, monetary

TABLE 4.2 *Inflation and the macroeconomic mix in selected sub-divisions of the OECD, 1972–81*

	Average annual rise in CPI	*Average annual rise in M1 plus quasi-money*	*Average annual rise in Real GDP*	*Average annual rise in M1 plus quasi money, less average annual rise in real GDP*	*Rise in percentage of total government outlays to GDP*	*Rise in percentage of total government current receipts to GDP*	*Net lending of government as percentage of GDP**		
	1972–81 (%)		*1972–81 (%)*		*1968–81*	*1968–81*	*1960–67 average*	*1968–73 average*	*1974–81 average*
Smaller countries	11.4	13.9	2.8	11.1	14.4	10.1	1.0	1.4	−0.8
OECD Europe	11.0	14.7	2.6	12.1	12.0	7.9	0.1	−0.1	−2.7
OECD less US	10.4	14.3	3.2	11.1	11.0	7.0	−0.2	0.1	−2.8
EEC	10.1	14.7	2.5	12.2	11.7	7.3	−0.2	−0.6	−3.3
All OECD	9.6	12.7	3.1	9.6	8.6	5.6	−0.1	0.1	−1.9
Major seven	9.1	12.5	3.1	9.4	7.6	4.8	−0.2	−0.1	−2.1
US	8.5	10.9	2.9	8.0	4.0	3.4	—	0.1	−0.1

* A negative figure signifies a budget deficit

Data so far available for 1982 indicate that the ranking of the groups would not be changed if the period covered had been extended to that date, except that OECD less US and the EEC had identical rises in *their* government outlay ratios for the period 1968–82.

SOURCE OECD, *Historical Statistics*.

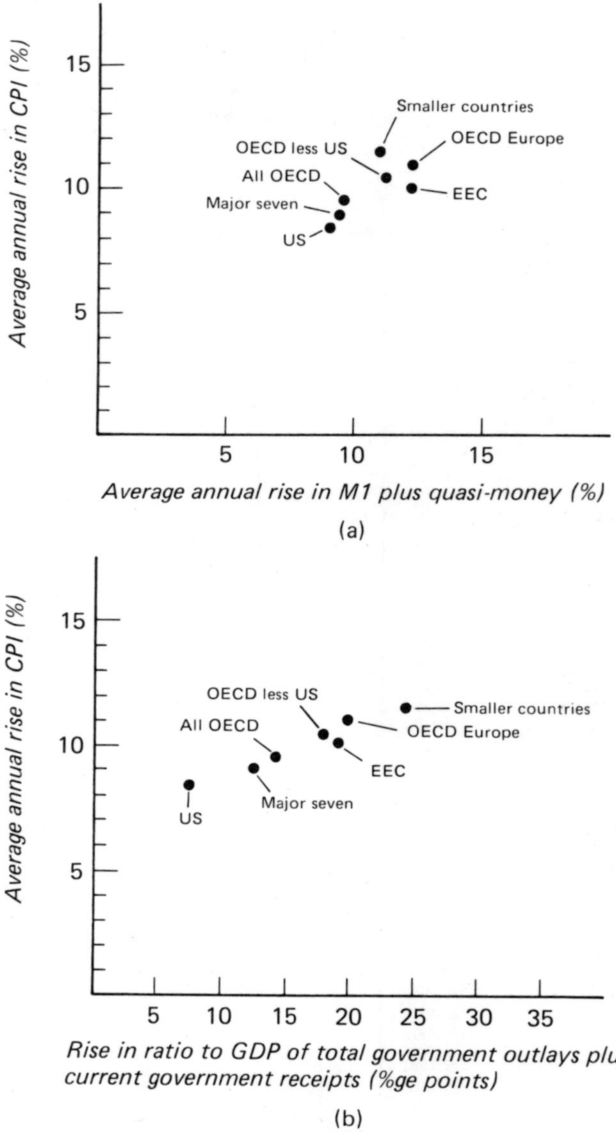

CHART 4.1 *Sub-divisions of OECD: inflation, government outlays and receipts, and monetary growth*

growth relative to real GDP growth was much less for the small-country group than for the three other groups with relatively high rates of inflation ($10\frac{3}{4}$%, compared with over $12\frac{1}{2}$%). There must therefore clearly be additional factors to be considered – quite apart from monetary growth – that might help to explain why relative rates of inflation for these various groups were as they were: a simple explanation in terms of monetary growth rates for the relative rates of inflation in the various groups is thus far from satisfactory.

BUDGETARY VARIABLES AND RELATIVE INFLATION

If, however, we introduce into the discussion the rises in the ratios of government receipts and outlays to GDP, as Table 4.2 also shows, we obtain an almost exact correspondence with the relative ranking of these sub-divisions in terms of their relative success (or failure) in holding down inflation. Indeed, their ranking in terms of the rise in the ratio of government current receipts to GDP or of total government outlays (and this is true also of total current disbursements, or of government consumption expenditure taken alone) to GDP is the same, with only one exception, as that for the sub-divisions in terms of their relative rates of inflation. The exception is that the EEC had a somewhat faster rate of increase in the various measures of government outlay and of receipts than did the OECD less the US (whereas the EEC had the higher rate of inflation of the two). It may be observed in passing that such a high degree of correspondence between the rise in the budgetary variables and inflation is remarkable; and in the present context it is worth emphasising that it is considerably closer to the ranking in terms of relative rates of inflation than is the ranking of these various sub-divisions in terms of either of the available measures of their monetary growth rates.*

It may also be observed that this ranking on the rise in the

* It does not appear that relative rates of increase in social security outlays played as significant a part (compared with other government outlays) – except in the sense that they were the most rapidly rising category of total government outlays. For the ranking of the various groupings in terms of the rise in the ratio of these outlays to GDP is appreciably less close to that for their relative rates of inflation than is the ranking on total government outlays, total current disbursements, or government consumption expenditure.

budgetary ratios implies that, for sub-divisions with approximately the same rate of monetary growth (OECD Europe compared with the EEC; the OECD total compared with the major seven; and the small-country group compared with the OECD total or the major seven), inflation tended to be higher in the groupings for which the rise in the budgetary ratios was relatively large. (This may be thought of as a very simple approximation to considering the way in which the settings of all these macroeconomic instruments interact in such a way as to influence the rate of inflation; a more sophisticated way of assessing this is to apply such econometric techniques as those used to compare the mix in the major seven countries that is used in Appendix 1 and referred to more fully in Chapter 5.)

BUDGET DEFICITS

In case it is suggested that the relative rise in government outlays may have been important merely because it could have tended to raise budget deficits; or that government current receipts rose relatively rapidly *merely as a result* of rising government outlays (so that one might have felt tempted to argue that the outlays rather than the taxes could might be said to influence the rate of inflation), it should be emphasised that, (as Table 4.2 also shows) the relative rise in budget deficits for these various groupings (as a proportion of their GDP) bore no such close relationship to their relative rates of inflation as did the rise in government current receipts, or even to that in government outlays. In particular, the group with the highest rates of inflation (the small countries) had one of the three *smallest* increases in budget deficits (relative to GDP) of any of the groupings between the average of 1960–67 and that of 1974–81; though it is true that, at the other extreme, the US, with the lowest rate of inflation, had the smallest relative rise in the budget deficit. But, in between, there appears to be no clear correlation between the rise in budget deficits (i.e. the fall in 'net lending' as shown in Table 4.3) and the rate of inflation for the various groups.

To summarise the experience of these groups it may be worth comparing the two simpler ways of disaggregating the OECD into only two (mutually exclusive) subdivisions: namely, the major seven compared with the group of smaller countries; and the US compared with the rest of the OECD.

THE MAJOR SEVEN AND THE SMALLER COUNTRIES

The rate of inflation was higher (and rose more) during these years for the small-country group, than in the major seven (taken as a group), despite the fact that monetary expansion (as measured by the OECD indicator of M1 plus quasi-money) relative to real GDP growth does not appear sufficient to explain why inflation was at a higher rate in the smaller countries than in the major seven.

For this reason, one may interpret the much faster rise in both current government receipts and total government outlays in the smaller countries than in the major seven as likely to have had a bearing on the much higher rate of inflation in the small-country group. Up to 1975 the ratio of government outlays to GDP for the smaller countries had been only about 2 percentage points above that for the major seven (and up to the end of the 1960s it had actually been lower); whereas between 1975 and 1980 it exceeded the corresponding ratio for the major seven by about 5–6 percentage points (on the average of those years). The ratio of current government receipts to GDP in the smaller countries had risen above that for the major seven in the mid-1960s, but was only slightly higher than theirs up to the later 1960s. But during the 1970s it rose progressively further above that for the major countries.

UNEMPLOYMENT AND THE MIX

Unemployment rose more in the smaller countries as a group than in the major seven; if higher unemployment was a factor tending to hold down inflation, this would make it harder to explain why the rate of inflation was higher in the smaller countries than in the major-country group, and thus makes it correspondingly more likely that their high and rising ratios of government outlays and receipts to GDP helps to explain their faster rate of inflation (see Table 4.3).

For the group of smaller countries, the much greater increase in the ratio of government outlays and receipts than for the other groups is clearly consistent with the view that a rising ratio of government outlays, and of government current receipts, to GDP makes it harder to hold down inflation in subsequent years at any given level of unemployment and with any given rate of increase in monetary aggregates.

TABLE 4.3 *Inflation, unemployment and budgetary ratios: groups of OECD countries*

(a)	*1967*	*1968*	*1969*	*1970*	*1971*
Rise in CPI (%)					
Major seven	2.7	4.1	5.0	5.7	5.0
Others	5.5	3.8	3.6	5.2	7.2
Unemployment					
Major seven	2.7	2.7	2.6	3.1	3.6
Others	4.0	4.2	4.1	4.2	4.3

(b)	*1967*	*1968*	*1969*	*1970*	*1971*	*1965–70*
Change in ratio of government current receipts to GDP (% of GDP)						
Major seven	0.5	1.1	1.0	–0.4	–0.3	2.8
Others	1.1	0.9	0.7	0.9	1.3	4.5
Change in ratio of total government outlays to GDP (% of GDP)						
Major seven	1.4	0.2	–0.2	0.6	0.4	2.7
Others	1.3	0.8	0.3	0.7	1.3	3.9

SOURCE OECD, *Historical Statistics: Economic Outlook.*

INFLATION AND THE MIX IN THE LATER 1960s

The strong association between a higher relative rate of inflation and more sharply rising tax rates and government outlay ratios in the small-country group could have been due, at least in part, to a tendency for high rates of inflation to raise the ratio of government receipts to GDP in the 1970s. But, even so far as that was true, this would not prevent a rise in that ratio from also making inflation worse (Nor, of course, would it mean that governments had to accept the rise in these ratios). Unfortunately, as both rates of inflation and sharp increases in these budgetary ratios were occurring together throughout most of the period, it is not easy to assess whether the causation was predominantly in one direction or the other.

In the later 1960s, however, as we have seen to be true of the OECD as a whole, the budgetary ratios were tending to rise sharply even before the rate of inflation increased appreciably in the later 1960s or early 1970s. Indeed, as Table 4.3 shows, those ratios were rising sharply for both these groups of countries during the period 1967–70, even though the rate of inflation was actually falling for the small-country group in 1968 and 1969 – so that the rising ratio of current government receipts to GDP in that period could for those countries not have been the *consequence* of higher inflation. Over the years 1968–70 the government outlay ratios for the small-country group rose by more than the corresponding ratios for the major-country group – even though the smaller countries had the lower rate of inflation; this difference could not therefore be reasonably interpreted as a *consequence* of their relative rates of inflation. From 1970 onwards, the continued rise in both budgetary ratios for the small-country group, relative to those for the major countries, was accompanied by consistently higher rates of inflation in the small-country group. This appears to be important additional evidence supporting the view that sharply rising budgetary ratios tend to be followed by correspondingly higher rates of inflation.

THE US AND THE WHOLE OF THE OECD

There is a case for giving attention to the comparison of the US with the rest of the OECD, which may be done indirectly for monetary growth back to the 1960s by taking the comparison of the US with the industrialised world as a whole. Data for monetary growth for the industrialised world are available from the IMF in a longer series than the OECD data (the IMF 'industrialised countries' group consisting of almost the same countries as the OECD), whilst the OECD data for monetary growth go back only to the early 1970s.

Inflation was generally at a lower rate in the US than in the rest of the OECD (taken as a whole) almost throughout the period under survey, the exception being the periods 1968–70 and 1979–80. The higher rate of inflation in the US in the later 1960s might be explained by various factors. There was a fall in unemployment there (without a comparable fall in the rest of the OECD), as well as a relative increase in monetary growth in the US (especially in relation to the rate of growth of real GDP in the US, which slowed down relative to the rest of the OECD). But, as Table 4.4 shows, there was also a rise in government current receipts in the US, and to a smaller extent in government outlays, at a time when the corresponding ratios for the

TABLE 4.4 *Unemployment, inflation and the macroeconomic mix 1967–71: US and total OECD*

	1967	*1968*	*1969*	*1970*	*1971*
Rise in CPI (%)					
US	2.8	4.2	5.4	5.9	4.3
Total OECD	3.1	4.1	4.8	5.6	5.3
Unemployment					
US	3.7	3.4	3.4	4.8	5.8
(% of labour force)					
Total OECD (i)	3.0	3.0	2.9	3.3	3.8
(ii)	2.7	2.8	2.6	3.0	3.6
Monetary growth (M1) (IMF definition)					
US	4.2	7.5	5.2	3.6	6.7
All industrialised countries	5.8	7.8	7.0	6.0	11.3
Rise in ratio of government current receipts					
US	0.4	1.7	1.2	−0.9	−0.7
to GDP (%ge of GDP)					
Total OECD	0.6	1.1	1.0	−0.3	−0.1
Rise in ratio of total government outlays to					
US	2.0	0.1	−0.4	1.4	0.0
GDP (%ge of GDP)					
Total OECD	1.4	0.3	−0.1	0.6	0.5

(i) Unadjusted unemployment rates for all countries
(ii) Standardised rates for fifteen countries

SOURCE OECD *Historical Statistics: Economic Outlook;* IMF, *International Financial Statistics*.

OECD as a whole were rising much less markedly (for virtually the only years during the entire period 1967–82).

The comparison of the US with the OECD as a whole during the last years of the 1960s is thus consistent with the view that rising ratios of government current receipts and outlays to GDP, as well as higher monetary growth rates (relative to real GDP growth), tend to raise inflation over the immediately subsequent years. But the experience would also be consistent with the view that lower unemployment, or higher monetary growth rates (alone) tend to make inflation worse. Either or both the mix hypothesis and the more orthodox monetarist or unemployment explanations would be consistent with this experience, and at this rather superficial level there is no obvious way to choose between them.

But it may well be significant that the ratio of government current receipts to GDP fell in the US in 1970 and 1971, whereas they continued to rise in the OECD as a whole. This change was followed by a reversal of the relative inflation rates – that of the US falling below that of the rest of the OECD from 1971 onwards (and remaining below it until 1979–80). The US showed a generally lower monetary growth rate than did the total for all industrialised countries; and the US also had a much smaller rate of increase than the OECD as a whole in the ratio of government outlays or receipts to GDP for the remainder of the period, taken as a whole.

In 1979–80, however, the rate of inflation in the US (as measured by the CPI, but not as measured by the implicit price index in the GDP deflator) rose above that in the rest of the OECD. One partial explanation for this may be that the level of unemployment in the US fell slightly in 1979, whereas that in the rest of the OECD continued to rise. But 1979–80 also followed a period of slower monetary growth in the US than in the rest of the US – though real GDP growth had also fallen away sharply in the US compared with the rest of the OECD. The experience of the US in 1979–80 is, however, also consistent with the view that rising tax rates tend to affect the rise in the price level in the years immediately following; for 1978 was the only year since 1972 when the ratio of current government receipts to GDP rose in the US while it was showing a fall for the rest of the OECD. On the other hand, the ratio of government outlays rose in 1978 much less in the US than in the rest of the OECD. Social security transfers, however, rose very sharply in the US in 1980, compared with the much smaller rise in the rest of the OECD.

In short, the above comparison of the US with the rest of the OECD is not conclusive as to whether the mix hypothesis performs better than the hypothesis that monetary growth or the level of unemployment explain relative rates of inflation; though the experience is certainly consistent with the mix hypothesis, and the mix hypothesis appears to be most obviously helpful for explaining the relative inflation rates during the period at the end of the 1960s – when inflation in the US rose above that in the rest of the OECD for the only time prior to 1979. But, as we have seen in earlier sections of this chapter, the more detailed comparisons of the US with various groupings of countries in the OECD, which are possible from the early 1970s (as it is from this date that the comparable monetary data for all these sub-divisions are available) does suggest that the mix hypothesis is more satisfactory as an explanation than are monetary growth rates alone, and far more satisfactory as an explanation than are relative increases in the level of unemployment.

BUDGETARY POLICY AND THE LEVEL OF ACTIVITY

Just as we saw in considering the experience of the OECD as a whole that the movement of the indicators of the macroeconomic policy mix over the period was generally in directions that could have been expected to make stagflation worse, and that this coincided with a general tendency for the overall setting of budgetary policy to be changed in directions that would tend to raise the level of unemployment (as Table 4.5 shows). This was true both of the US and of the major seven as a group during the period 1975–79. But as Table 4.6 shows, during the early 1980s the readiness of the US to provide a stimulus partly by tax cuts combined with a tight monetary policy (and despite high and rising levels of many inflationary forms of government outlay, notably defence spending) stood in marked contrast to the policies of most OECD governments throughout the period; and it was marked by conspicuous success in reducing both unemployment and inflation – which is the outcome that the analysis presented above would have led one to expect.

We may conclude, therefore, that, as with the OECD as a whole, relative macroeconomic success in the major sub-divisions into which the OECD data can be disaggregated was influenced both by the mix of macroeconomic instruments and by the overall setting of budgetary policy; and that failure to select the sort of macroeconomic mix that was most likely to hold down the price level at any given level of employment tended to cause governments to make their overall policy, or at least their budgetary policy, relatively deflationary.

TABLE 4.5 *General government structural budget balance, with and without inflation adjustment: US and the other six major countries, 1973–82 (% of GDP)*

	1973	*1974*	*1975*	*1976*	*1977*	*1978*	*1979*	*1980*	*1981*	*1982*
With inflation adjustment										
US	1.6	3.2	2.3	1.7	2.0	2.5	3.6	3.5	3.7	1.7
Other six	0.3	0.8	–0.5	–0.6	–0.1	–2.3	–1.5	–1.0	0.3	0.2
Without inflation adjustment										
US	0.2	0.6	–0.8	0.3	0.4	0.7	1.0	0.7	1.4	0.3
Other six	–0.8	–1.0	–3.0	–2.9	–2.5	–3.8	–3.7	–3.0	–2.6	–1.5

Positive figures as *contractionary*
Negative figures are *expansionary*

These figures are very approximate, having been read off Chart G, OECD *Economic Outlook*, Dec. 1983.

The balances without the inflation adjustment are the actual figures for the budget balance adjusted only for the effects of cyclical factors.

The balances with the inflation adjustment allow also for the additional budget surplus that results so far as inflation reduces the real value of the national debt.

TABLE 4.6 *Change in general government structural balance, US and major seven OECD countries, 1975–79 and 1979–82 as percentage of GDP*

	1975–79		*1979–82*	
	Without inflation adjustment	*With inflation adjustment*	*Without inflation adjustment*	*With inflation adjustment*
US	+2.1	+2.8	–0.9	–1.7
Total Major seven	+0.7	+0.6	+0.5	+0.1

A positive movement is *contractionary* and a negative movement is *expansionary*

SOURCE OECD; data for 1981 and 1982 are published in OECD *Economic Outlook*, July 1984; data for earlier years communicated by the OECD.

5 The Major Seven

This chapter discusses the evidence of the policy mix in the seven largest OECD economies, the United States, Japan, Germany, France, Britain, Italy and Canada, and of its relationship to their relative macroeconomic success during the period from the later 1960s to the early 1980s.

The approach of the two preceding chapters, involving the aggregation of data from a number of countries, may suffer from the limitation that conclusions drawn from this aggregate data might have been a chance result of the aggregation: for the countries with less macroeconomic success within a particular group might not be the same as those that had a macroeconomic policy setting that could have been expected to produce the relative lack of macroeconomic success.

On the other hand, the case of every individual country is obviously likely to be greatly influenced by considerations quite distinct from the policy mix; indeed, the tendency for every country to believe that its own circumstances are distinctive (or even unique) has probably done much to cause inadequate attention to be paid to those deficiencies in the macroeconomic mix which have been of significance in virtually all of them – but which tend to be dominated by other factors when the experience of any individual country is being considered.

INFLATION AND UNEMPLOYMENT IN THE MAJOR SEVEN

The policies of the countries for much of the period from the late 1960s to the early 1980s was apparently based on the implicit assumption that high unemployment helped to restrain inflation and that there was no available means to achieve the same effect that did not involve the creation or continuation of the high unemployment. But if this assumption were valid one would expect there to be some association between high or rising levels of unemployment and low rates of inflation. This section considers whether there is any clear tendency for those major OECD countries that permitted high levels of unemployment also to have relatively low rates of inflation.

There is obviously no such relationship between inflation and unemployment for Japan and Germany, the two countries that were most successful in maintaining a relatively high degree of macroeconomic achievement during the 1970s. For, as Table 5.1 shows, these two countries had by far the lowest average rate of unemployment over the whole period, whereas Germany also had the lowest average rate of inflation; and Japan's rate of inflation was below the OECD average for the period since 1973 (though well above it up to the early 1970s). Moreover, for the second half of the 1970s (taken alone), during which Japan and Germany had clearly the lowest average unemployment rates of the seven, they had also a lower inflation rate than the other major OECD countries. So far from being consistent with the hypothesis that high rates of unemployment help to keep down the rate of inflation, this evidence would suggest the exact contrary.

At the other extreme, the two highest rates of inflation for the period 1971–82 were shown by Italy and Britain. Over the whole period these two countries had also the two highest registered unemployment rates among the European major countries. Again, this evidence would be consistent with the view that *high* rates of unemployment and *high* rates of inflation tend to go together – rather than providing any justification for the reverse proposition (which would be necessary to provide a basis for the view that inflation can be checked only by permitting high unemployment).

On the other hand, it might perhaps be said of the three remaining countries, the United States, France and Canada, that relatively high unemployment rates and relatively low inflation rates tended to some extent to go together (within the group in question). For, of these three, France had both the *highest* rate of inflation and the *lowest* level of registered unemployed, whilst the United States and Canada had approximately the same rate of both inflation and registered unemployed as one another – though the US had a slightly lower rate of *both* inflation and unemployment. Again, this would be highly questionable evidence on which to base policies of tolerating high unemployment in the hope of thereby restraining inflation; and, taking the evidence from the experience of these countries, it might with more justice be invoked to support the opposite view that low unemployment may tend to keep inflation down.

TABLE 5.1 *Unemployment and inflation: major seven OECD countries*

	Rise in CPI (% per annum)							*Unemployment (% of labour force)*			
	1967	*1968*	*1969*	*1970*	*1971–82 average*	*1982*	*Fall from 1970s peak to 1982*	*1967*	*1982*	*Change 1967–82*	*1970–82*
Italy	3.7	1.4	2.6	5.0	14.7	16.6	4.6	5.3	8.9	+3.6	+3.6
Britain	2.5	4.7	5.4	6.4	13.2	8.6	15.6	3.3	12.8	+9.5	+8.8
France	2.7	4.5	6.4	5.2	10.2	11.8	1.9	1.9	8.0	+6.1	+5.6
Canada	3.6	4.0	4.5	3.4	8.7	10.8	0.1	3.8	10.9	+7.1	+5.3
Japan	4.0	5.3	5.2	7.7	8.2	2.7	21.8	1.3	2.4	+1.1	+1.3
US	2.8	4.2	5.4	5.9	7.9	6.1	7.4	3.7	9.5	+5.8	+4.7
Germany	1.4	2.9	1.9	3.4	5.2	5.3	1.7	1.3	6.1	+4.8	+5.3

In short, the evidence of a comparison between these seven countries is that there is no clear association between relatively high inflation rates and relatively low unemployment. The evidence provided by this sort of comparison of the experience of these countries thus certainly affords no support for policies of trying to restrain inflation by tolerating high unemployment as a means of achieving macroeconomic success.

Perhaps one might be tempted to use this simple evidence to support the opposite view – namely, that holding *down* unemployment tends to *reduce* inflation. But a more justifiable conclusion would be that the relationship between inflation, on the one hand, and high unemployment, on the other, is not a clear-cut one in either direction, partly because the policy mix accompanying the unemployment will determine its effect on inflation.

Furthermore, there are also other good *a priori* reasons why this should be so. For, on the one hand, there is the effect most widely thought to be true – that lower levels of unemployment usually encourage higher wage settlements and more rapid price increases; but, on the other hand, there is also the less widely discussed countervailing consideration that when industry is operating well below capacity its unit costs rise, and this factor tends to raise average costs, and to that extent prices.

This is also true of the important overheads for the economy as a whole that take the form of government outlays on the public service, defence and so on; and a good deal of the country's communications system. The lower is the output of the economy the higher must tax rates and charges be per unit of output to finance these 'social' overheads; and the consequently higher tax rates and government charges raise the price level from the cost side. (One way of reducing the ratios would thus be to permit business activity to recover.) The further an economy is below capacity the greater the likelihood that this consideration that recession raises unit costs will predominate over any tendency for high unemployment to hold down wage and price increases; so that one might have expected that the low levels of activity in the later 1970s and early 1980s would have led to upward pressure on unit costs, and to that extent to greater upward pressure on prices – on a scale that could well in some countries and periods have exceeded whatever effect the low levels of output and employment may have had in restraining wage and price increases through the level of demand. (A more sophisticated test of the relationship between unemployment and inflation in these countries, over the period 1967–82, is reported in Appendix 1; it is consistent with the view that there is no clear relationship either way between inflation and unemployment, in that the explanation of the rate of inflation in a given year in these countries that is provided by changes in their respective macroeconomic mixes over the preceding two years is not improved upon by the addition of unemployment as a further factor.)

CHANGES IN INFLATION AND UNEMPLOYMENT

If the hypothesis is not that the relative *level* of registered unemployed needs to be high in order to bring about a low level of inflation, but that readiness to *increase* unemployment helps to hold down the rate of inflation, again the evidence from comparing the figures for these seven countries is certainly not clearly – if at all – in favour of the proposition.

The rise in unemployment in Japan between 1970 and 1982 was (as Table 5.1 shows) the *lowest* among these seven countries, whereas the rate of inflation in Japan was also the *lowest* in the last years of the period; and the fall from its peak rate of inflation was the largest among the seven. Moreover, the rise in unemployment in Britain was clearly the largest among the seven, but its rate of inflation had by 1982 been brought down only to about the average of the seven, though the fall from its peak rate was the second-largest. It is true that Italy showed the smallest rise in registered unemployment over the period, as well as the fastest rate of inflation (and one of the smallest reduotions in it from its peak rate). On the other hand, inflation in the US was third-*lowest*, yet the rise in unemployment over the period in that country was less than the average for the seven. France had the second highest rate of inflation and the second biggest rise in unemployment, but a very small reduction in inflation from its peak rate. This very confused picture is certainly nowhere near the convincing evidence that one would require in order to support the view that increases in unemployment were both necessary and sufficient to reduce inflation to relatively low levels; and some of the evidence suggests that countries that successfully held down inflation (relative to the others) were also relatively successful in holding down the rise in unemployment.

Of course, this evidence does not imply that a rise in unemployment will necessarily do nothing to hold down inflation – nor that a rise in unemployment tends to make inflation worse. The right conclusion from this limited evidence should be that it does not provide any support for the view that either high or relatively sharply rising unemployment can be expected *of itself* to make a country more successful than other comparable countries in restraining inflation. Yet to justify policies that tolerate high unemployment with a view to checking inflation one would logically require convincing evidence that a policy of tolerating high or increasing unemployment would *in itself* restrain inflation – irrespective of the mix whereby it was achieved; *and* that it would succeed better in achieving that aim than would any alternative policies, such as a change of mix at given (or a higher) level of employment. Higher unemployment with the right mix can reduce inflation; but with the wrong mix it can make inflation worse.

MACRO INSTRUMENTS AND MACROECONOMIC SUCCESS IN THE MAJOR SEVEN

When the experience of the principal groupings of OECD countries was considered in the previous chapter, there was found to be a very clear association between their relative rates of inflation, on the one hand, and rises in the level of their tax rates, of their government outlay ratios, and of the setting of their monetary policies, on the other. There is no such obvious association between the main indicators of the mix in each of the major seven and their relative success in restraining inflation; much more complex ways of examining the data are required in order to ascertain whether such an association exists – and this is attempted in the Appendix (p. 113).

But, as Table 5.2 shows, there is a clear tendency for monetary growth rates to be high in the countries where inflation rates are also relatively high, and for real interest rates to be low in those countries where inflation was greatest. France had a slightly higher rate of inflation than Canada, though France had a lower monetary growth rate (but much greater rises in the budgetary ratios).

Some of the budgetary indicators also tend to confirm the basic hypothesis – even at this level of casual observation. In particular, the two North American countries had relatively low levels of government outlays and receipts, and relatively small increases in them over the period as a whole, compared with most of the other major OECD countries that had higher rates of inflation than the two North American countries.

TABLE 5.2 *Inflation and the macroeconomic mix, major seven OECD countries, 1972–82*

	Rise in CPI % per annum 1972–82 average	*Rise in M1 plus quasi-money less rise in real GDP % per annum 1972–82 average*		*Real-long term bond rate % 1972–82 average*	*Rise in ratio to GDP of*	
		IMF	*OECD*		*government current receipts*	*total government outlays*
Italy	15.4	15.7	14.4	−2.0	10.6	15.1
Britain	13.5	14.7	14.9	−0.9	6.9	7.6
France	9.8	11.1	11.0	+1.1	8.7	12.4
Canada	9.2	12.6	13.2	+0.5	3.1	8.6
Japan	8.4	8.7	8.2	+1.5	8.7	12.7
US	8.3	6.4	8.3	+1.1	2.0	5.6
Germany	5.2	6.3	6.7	+3.1	5.5	8.6

SOURCE OECD, *Economic Outlook: Historical Statistics;* IMF, *International Financial Statistics.*

On the hand, the two most successful countries – Japan and Germany – had either sharply rising, though low (Japan), or relatively high and sharply rising (Germany) ratios of government outlays and current receipts to GDP, although their relatively low rates of monetary growth (in relation to the rate of growth of real GDP) and high real interest rates presumably tended to reduce the upward pressure on the price level that would otherwise have resulted from the rising budgetary ratios in Japan and Germany.

The upshot of this brief discussion is that there appears to be a clear tendency for relatively tight monetary policies to be associated with greater success in restraining inflation; but that – at this casual level of observation, and on the basis of this evidence – one cannot judge whether holding down government outlays and tax receipts also helps to reduce the upward pressure on the price level. The monetary policy indicators thus appear to have been more obviously significant than the budgetary ratios.

But when the data are analysed in a more sophisticated manner there is (as shown in the Appendix, p. 113) a clear tendency for increases in the ratio of government outlays and current receipts to GDP over a period of two years to be associated with relatively sharp rises in the consumer price index in these countries in the succeeding year.

There is no reason to be surprised that this tendency is not evident from a superficial look at the tables – such as was sufficient for the purpose when looking at the main groupings of OECD countries. For each individual country is naturally subject to many special influences – including those that affect the state of its balance of payments, and such influences as the presence or absence of a successful prices and incomes policy – that may have an important bearing upon its macroeconomic success (with any given macroeconomic mix). These features that are distinctive for each country tend to average out when looking at relatively large groups of them (as was done in the previous chapter), whereas more sophisticated forms of averaging are necessary in order to draw general conclusions from the experience of the individual countries.

Moreover, the conclusions to be drawn can be held with much greater confidence when such forms of analysis are used in such a way as to assess simultaneously the relative contributions of each of the macroeconomic instruments simultaneously (rather than each of them separately – as was in practice the approach adopted in the previous chapters).

CHANGES IN THE MIX IN TWO SUB-PERIODS

The preceding broad survey of the relative macroeconomic success of the seven major OECD countries over the period as a whole may be complemented by a discussion of their respective policies in two particular periods: the first is the changes in their mix of macroeconomic measures in the late 1960s – the period when unemployment and inflation began to rise simultaneously; and the second is the later 1970s, when they were all faced by the problem of holding down inflation, and in varying degrees handled it by policy measures that involved very sharp rises in unemployment (far in excess of those occurring in any earlier period since World War II). The period from the early 1970s until about 1975 is so dominated by the oil price changes that references to changes in the policy mix alone do not provide a ready explanation of relative macroeconomic success during the period. But the analysis of the Appendix (p. 113) makes allowance for changes in the oil price over the whole period and shows the relationship between rates of inflation and changes in the macroeconomic mix after allowing for the oil price changes.

THE LATE 1960s

Between 1967 and 1970 the annual rise in the CPI for the major seven as a group increased by three percentage points. The *rise* for the US was less than for the major seven as a group, but for the three years 1968–70 the actual rate of inflation in the US was on this measure greater than for the rest of the major seven – in contrast to the generally lower rates of inflation in the US both in previous years and in later years of the 1970s (apart from 1979 and 1980).

As Table 5.3 shows, over the course of those later years of the 1960s Japan had by far the highest rate of inflation of the seven, followed by Britain and France. Germany had by far the lowest rate of inflation over this period.

Changes in unemployment rates do not seem to provide a ready explanation of the relative rates of inflation, or of changes in them. Germany and Italy, with the two *lowest* rates of inflation over the period (and, for Germany, also the smallest rise between the mid-1960s and 1970), showed a tendency for unemployment to *fall*, whereas for the others it was stable or rising.

Furthermore, as Table 5.3 also shows, relative rates of inflation in

TABLE 5.3 *Inflation, unemployment and the policy mix: major seven OECD countries, later 1960s and 1970*

	Rise in CPI (%)		*Change in unemployment* (as % of labour force) 1967–70*	*Annual rise in M1 plus quasi-money less annual rise in real GDP, 1967–70 (% per annum)*		*Change in ratio to GDP between 1965 and 1970 of*	
	1967–70 average	*Change from 1967 to 1970*		*OECD*	*IMF*	*Government current receipts*	*Total government outlays*
Japan	5.5	+3.7	−0.2	5.0	5.0	+1.2	−0.7
Britain	4.8	+3.9	−0.2	5.0	n.a.	+7.1	+2.8
France	4.7	+2.5	+0.5	6.5	4.7	+0.6	+0.5
US	4.6	+3.1	+1.1	5.2	3.9	+3.1	+4.5
Canada	3.9	−0.2	+1.8	n.a.	6.6	+7.1	+6.6
Italy	3.2	+1.3	0.0	6.2	6.6	+0.3	−0.1
Germany	2.4	+2.0	−0.5	6.6	6.7	+2.6	+2.1

*OECD standardised figures
'n.a.' signifies 'not available'

SOURCE OECD, *Historical Statistics, Economic Outlook*; IMF *International Financial Statistics Yearbook*, 1983.

that period cannot readily be explained in terms of monetary growth rates. In particular, Britain, which had one of the two *highest* rates of inflation, and one of the largest increases in it over the period, had one of the two *lowest* monetary growth rates in this period of the later 1960s (both in absolute terms and also allowing for relative rates of growth in real GDP). At the other extreme, Italy, with one of the two *lowest* rates of inflation in the later 1960s, and also the *lowest* increase in it (for Canada the rate actually fell) over the period, had one of the three *fastest* monetary growth rates relative to the rate of growth of real GDP. Clearly, an explanation in terms of relative monetary growth rates for the respective rates of inflation of the major seven (or for the rises in them) over this period is highly unconvincing (just as we saw above that an explanation in terms of changes in the level of unemployment is also unconvincing).

But the high rate of inflation in Britain, and its increase over the second half of the 1960s (which was exceeded only by that of Japan), may be partly explained by the fact that the ratio of government current receipts to GDP in Britain rose between 1965 and 1970 more than that for any of the other major seven, so that by 1970 that ratio for Britain was in excess of that for any other major OECD country. The ratio of total government outlays to GDP in Britain had also come by 1970 to exceed that for any other major OECD country, though its average level for the years 1968–70 was about the same as that for France and Germany.

Relative rates of increase in the budgetary variables may also help to explain, at the other extreme, the relative success of Italy in holding down its rate of inflation in the face of its very high monetary growth rate. For the ratio of government current receipts to GDP for Italy rose only very slightly (less than for any other major OECD country); and the ratio of government outlays to GDP in Italy was stable or falling over that period.

It is true that casual observation of this sort cannot properly indicate the way in which changes in the setting of the main macro-economic instruments may help to explain the relative rises in inflation rates among the major seven; but it can certainly be concluded that relative changes in unemployment and monetary growth rates (alone) do not appear to afford convincing explanations; and that relative changes in the ratio of government outlays and receipts to GDP appear to be capable of helping to explain at least some of the relative changes in inflation rates. The evidence is certainly consistent with the view that each of these main elements in the mix does matter

– in the sense of influencing the extent of the upward pressure on the price level at any given level of employment; and the evidence considered above is *not* consistent with the view that relative unemployment rates, or relative monetary growth rates, *alone* (or together), can help to explain changes in relative inflation rates among the major seven in this period of the later 1960s, when stagflation may reasonably be said to have begun to take hold of their economies.

If this sort of evidence had been considered in this light when it first became available, and if the lessons for policy that they imply had been properly absorbed into accepted thinking, it seems unlikely that governments would have adopted during the 1970s the combinations of rising government outlays and current receipts (relative to GDP), coupled with relatively rapid monetary growth and low or negative real interest rates that characterised most of the 1970s – or that they would have tolerated such high unemployment, in the hope of thereby checking the inflation that resulted from those mixes.

CHANGES IN THE MIX BETWEEN 1975 AND 1982

From the mid-1970s onwards the major seven OECD countries all tried to handle the problem of high rates of inflation partly by tolerating high and rising levels of unemployment; but they did so with varying mixes of tax rates, government outlays and government policies.

As Table 5.4 shows, it was not the countries that tolerated the greatest rise, or the highest average level, of unemployment that were most successful in checking inflation. Indeed, the two countries with the lowest rates of inflation over the period, Japan and Germany, had two of the three lowest increases in unemployment; and Britain, with the second highest average inflation rate, had by far the largest rise in unemployment. There seems to be no clear correlation between these countries' respective success in restraining inflation and either the level, or the extent of the increase in, their unemployment.

But the changes in the setting of their macroeconomic mixes does appear to have had a bearing on their relative success over this period. In particular, as Table 5.4 also shows, there is a very close relationship between their average monetary growth rate (on the basis of the OECD figures for 'M1 plus quasi-money') and their relative rates of inflation. Indeed, the ranking of the seven countries is, with only one exception, the same for their inflation rates as for

TABLE 5.4 *Inflation, unemployment and the macroeconomic mix: major seven OECD countries, 1975–82*

	Rise in CPI % per annum 1975–82 average	Change in annual CPI rise % 1975–82	Unemployment as % of labour force*		Rise in M1 plus quasi-money less rise in real GDP % per annum 1975–82	Rise in ratio to GDP of	
			Change 1975–82	Average 1975–82		government current receipts % 1975–82	total government outlays % 1975–82
Italy	17.0	–0.4	3.1	7.3	16.7	10.3	10.5
Britain	14.6	–15.6	7.7	7.4	13.3	3.2	0.8
France	11.2	0	3.9	5.7	10.7	6.6	7.2
Canada	9.7	0	4.0	7.9	12.2	3.1	5.0
US	8.8	–3.0	1.2	7.3	8.6	2.3	2.0
Japan	6.5	–9.1	0.5	2.1	6.6	6.2	7.2
Germany	4.7	–0.7	2.5	3.9	5.5	2.7	0.5

*Standardised by OECD.

SOURCE OECD, *Historical Statistics: Economic Outlook.*

their monetary growth rates (allowing for their relative growth rates of real GDP). Moreover, the country with the highest rate of inflation, Italy, has about three times as high a rate of inflation as the one with the lowest, Germany, and also had three times the (adjusted) monetary growth rate; whilst France and Canada, with inflation rates about twice that of Germany, had just about twice the adjusted monetary growth rate of Germany.

But, in addition, the changes in the budgetary ratios appear to have had some bearing on the relative extent of inflation in the different countries. Italy, with the highest rate of inflation, showed the biggest rises in both budgetary ratios; and Germany, with the lowest rate of inflation, showed the smallest rises in these ratios. Moreover, in the one case where a country with a higher rate of inflation than another had the lower adjusted monetary growth rate of the two, the higher inflation rate in France than in Canada (despite the lower monetary growth rate in France) may reasonably be attributed in part to the greater rise in the budgetary ratios for France.

1979–82

In the last few years of the period the United States pursued a somewhat different policy from the rest of the major seven, at any rate at the end of that period, in the sense that its budget moved in an expansionary direction, mainly as a result of tax cuts, whilst monetary policy was kept tight. The experience of these years thus constitutes something of a case study of a policy that was in certain respects like that being suggested in the present study – except that the considerable rise in the ratio of government outlays to GDP in the US is not consistent with a mix that would, a priori, have been the sort most likely to minimise stagflation.

Table 5.5a shows that during the period 1979–82, when unemployment was rising rapidly in the OECD as a whole, only the US and Italy showed a net change in the setting of their budgets in a direction tending to reduce unemployment – with Italy showing a much smaller expansionary movement than the US if allowance is made for the contractionary effect of inflation in reducing the real value of the national debt.

By contrast, the budgetary settings of all the other major OECD countries were moving in a direction tending to make unemployment worse than it would otherwise have been, with Britain showing a

TABLE 5.5a *Change in general government structural balance as percentage of GDP: major OECD countries, 1979–82*

	Without inflation adjustment	*With inflation adjustment*
US	−0.9	−1.7
Italy	−1.5	−0.2
Canada	+0.4	+0.7
France	+0.6	+1.0
Germany	+1.4	+1.7
Japan	+1.6	+1.7
Britain	+7.6	+4.1
Total major seven	+0.5	+0.1

A positive movement is *contractionary* and a negative movement *expansionary*

SOURCE OECD. Data for 1980 and 1981 published in OECD *Economic Outlook*, July, 1984; data for earlier years communicated to the author by OECD.

TABLE 5.5b *Change in government outlays and current receipts as percentage of GDP: major OECD countries, 1979–82*

	(1) Rise in government outlays	*(2) Rise in government current receipts*	*(3) (1) + (2)*
Germany	1.8	1.6	2.8
US	4.6	0.3	4.9
Japan	2.9	3.6	6.5
France	5.2	3.2	8.4
Britain	4.2	5.0	9.2
Canada	6.5	2.9	9.4
Italy	8.2	5.8	14.0
Total major seven	3.7	1.4	5.1

SOURCE OECD, *Economic Outlook*.

much more marked movement in that direction than any of the others. Yet the rise in unemployment in Britain – of some seven percentage points on the OECD standardised basis – was much greater than for any other OECD country, which would seem to indicate a need for budgetary policy in Britain to have been *more* expansionary than elsewhere; and to imply that budgetary policy in Britain over that period was making the net outcome for unemployment there appreciably worse.

For the major seven as a whole, there was only a small net change in budgetary policy in a contractionary direction; and without the large contractionary movement in Britain the net movement for the seven would have been expansionary, as the net stimulatory effect of the change in the budget in the US exceeded the contractionary effect of the budgetary policies of the other major countries apart from Britain (taken as a group).

Table 5.5b shows that the much more expansionary movement in the budgetary policy of the US (compared with the rest of the major seven) resulted mainly from the fact that the ratio of government current receipts to GDP there rose only slightly over the period (and it actually fell in 1982), rather than mainly because of the rise in government outlays, though these also rose rather more, in relation to GDP, than for the major seven as a whole.

The other major country whose budget moved in an expansionary direction over the period, Italy, showed by far the biggest rise in both government outlays and current receipts in relation to GDP.

At the other extreme, Britain, whose budget moved furthest in a contractionary direction over the period, showed one of the three largest increases in government outlays and receipts taken together, and a rise in government current receipts second only to that for Italy.

Of the three other countries who also moved their budgets over the period in a contractionary direction (as indicated in Table 5.5a) – France, Germany and Japan – Germany clearly did so with the least inflationary combination of government outlays and receipts, as its government outlays rose relatively less than for any other major country, and its government current receipts rose relatively less than for any except the US (and the two budgetary ratios together less than for any other major OECD country).

But the other two countries with contractionary changes in their budgetary policies, Japan and France, showed much sharper rises in the two budgetary ratios than did Germany – though less than for Britain, Canada or Italy.

Canada, whose budgetary policy also moved somewhat in a contractionary direction over the period, effected that policy with sharply rising ratios of both government outlays and current receipts to GDP, the two ratios together rising by more than for any major country except Italy.

In short, to the contractionary effect of the movement of their budgets (as indicated by the cyclically adjusted changes in the budget outturn) should be added the contractionary effect that these increasing budgetary ratios would have through their upward pressure on the price level and consequent reduction in the real value of the stock of money. That effect was especially relevant for Britain, Canada and France, and negated at least part of the expansionary effect of the movement of the budget for Italy. That cost-increasing effect was much less for the US, Germany and Japan. But the policy of the US in 1981–82, showed that it is possible to bring about a very sharp recovery, whilst still holding down the rate of inflation by way of tax cuts accompanied by fairly tight monetary policy.

This conclusion requires special emphasis in view of the highly misguided tendency of many governments to justify tight *budgetary* measures on the grounds that they will help to hold down *monetary* expansion; whereas if monetary restraint is the aim of policy, the monetary policy instruments are the appropriate ones to use in order to achieve it.

In short, the evidence of the major seven over this period since the middle of the 1970s is consistent with the view that it is most likely that the setting of macroeconomic instruments that will do most to facilitate the achievement of the main macroeconomic aims is to use monetary policy to hold down the growth of monetary aggregates, whilst the budget is set in a reasonably expansionary direction (after making due allowance for cyclical factors) *by way of tax cuts*.

It thus constitutes a serious obstacle to the proper setting of monetary and budgetary policy if the running of budget deficits (or more expansionary budgetary policies generally) is regarded as an obstacle to keeping '*monetary* policy' tight; for confusion of the control of *monetary aggregates* with the *instruments of monetary policy*, often leads governments to employ budgetary measures – especially higher taxes – principally with the aim of trying to curtail *monetary growth*.

It should be stressed that the particular combination of budgetary measures with which a stimulus is given is no less important than the matter of whether budgetary policy is sufficiently expansionary to hold down unemployment; and, by the same token, when economic recovery enables a government to reduce the extent of budgetary stimulus it will be no less important to do this in ways that minimise the risk of contributing to cost-inflation – in other words, it will be important to reduce the stimulus, when the time comes, primarily by restraint in government outlays rather than by raising tax rates. The evidently greater success of those countries that restrained monetary growth and also held down the rise in their budgetary ratios should provide clear support for policy mixes that incorporate the lessons of those countries' experience.

But it should be noted that the particular combination of taxation and government outlays that is employed to make the setting of the budget expansionary is also likely to be important. For in Japan taxes and government outlays were rising relative to real GDP, but were still relatively low compared with the average of the other countries, and in Germany tax rates were not exceptionally high if allowance is made for the high real income per head of Germany compared with most of the other major countries. Moreover, after cyclical adjustment, tax rates in Japan and Germany would have risen considerably less by comparison with the other countries in the group than did their unadjusted tax rates (because the latter had generally higher and more sharply rising unemployment rates than did Japan and Germany); and, by contrast, if allowance is made for cyclical factors, tax rates (and, still more so, government outlays) in Italy rose in relation to GDP by rather more than the unadjusted ratios (to judge from the estimates made by the IMF that are summarised in Table 5.5).

THE 'REAL-WAGE GAP', 1972–81

The OECD has frequently (in its twice-yearly *Economic Outlook*) analysed the rise in real wage rates in manufacturing in principal member countries in relation to productivity growth since a base-year. Various observers have suggested that a rising 'real-wage gap' in this sense may have contributed to the macroeconomic problems of the 1970s and early 1980s.*

The present section considers whether those countries among the major seven that had the most rapid rise in real wage rates relative to productivity growth, first in 1972–75, and then over the longer period 1972–81, were those in which the changes in the macroeconomic mix were such as to be likely to raise money wage rates at any given level of economic activity. A relatively easy setting of monetary policy may make employers readier to give into wage demands, and high tax

*See, for example, Corden (1981).

rates on wage and salary-earners, and the diversion of relatively large shares of available output into government purchases, rather than into marketable goods and services, make wage and salary-earners demand greater rises in their pre-tax incomes; and, if employers cannot fully pass on the wage increases by way of higher prices, this can clearly result in real wages rising faster than productivity – so that one could, on those assumptions, expect the 'real-wage gap' to gape most widely in those countries and periods where the ratios of government outlays and current receipts were rising most sharply, and where the setting of monetary policy was easiest. This is not to argue that the rise in real wage rates (relative to available real output) was entirely due to the inappropriate setting of the macroeconomic mix; but, clearly, if there is a presumption that the mix played a part in leading to the rise of real (as well as money) wage rates this is an important consideration in determining future policy. As we shall see below, it does appear that the problem of the 'real-wage gap' generally loomed largest in those countries and periods where the changes in the macroeconomic mix tended to be in directions that one could have expected to make inflation (including wage inflation) worse at any given level of employment.

Between 1972 and 1975 there were (as Table 5.6 shows) sharp rises in real wage rates (in manufacturing) relative to productivity (adjusted for changes in the terms of trade of the country concerned) in all the major seven countries except the US. By far the largest rises in 'real wages' (as defined in this way) over that period occurred in Japan, Britain and France; the rise in Italy was rather less; and it was very much lower in Canada and Germany. It was so slight as to be negligible in the US.

To the best of the knowledge of the present writer, the relative rises in real wage rates over the period have not been considered against the preceding changes in the macroeconomic mix to see whether it is likely that the rises in the real-wage gap were attributable (wholly or partly) to an unsound setting of the mix of macroeconomic policy. Yet the evidence for such an association seems clear when the relative changes in real wages in these various countries are compared with the indicators of the changes in the setting of the main macroeconomic instruments in each of these countries over the immediately preceding years.

In the first place, monetary growth rates were highest (relative to the growth of real GDP in each country) over the period (over the

TABLE 5.6 *Real-wage gaps: major seven, 1972–75 and 1972–81*

	Rise in real wages less productivity growth adjusted for terms of trade 1972–75 (% per annum)	*Rise in M1 plus quasi-money less real GDP growth (% per annum)*		*Rise in ratios to GDP 1970–75 (% of GDP)*		
		1970–73	*1970–75*	*Government current receipts (a)*	*Total government outlays (b)*	*(a) + (b)*
Japan	4.2	22.7	17.8	3.3	7.8	11.1
Britain	3.8	16.6	19.5	0.1	7.6	7.7
France	3.1	16.7	16.8	1.3	4.6	5.9
Italy	2.2	18.0	18.5	0.8	9.0	9.8
Canada	1.7	15.2*	16.4*	1.7	5.1	6.8
Germany	1.4	14.0	10.2	4.2	10.3	14.3
US	0.3	12.3	11.2	0.2	3.2	3.4

	Rise in real wages less rise in productivity adjusted for terms of trade (1981–82 as of 1972)	Rise in M1 plus quasi-money less rise in real GDP (% per annum) 1972–81	Rise in ratio to GDP (% of GDP) 1972–81: Government current receipts	Total government outlays	
			(a)	(b)	(a) + (b)
France	111¾	10.9	7.9	10.6	18.5
Italy	109¼	15.9	7.8	12.2	20.0
Japan	108¼	8.0	7.8	12.0	19.8
Canada	106¾	13.7	2.8	4.2	7.0
US	102¾	8.2	2.9	3.4	6.3
Germany	100	6.9	4.7	8.4	13.1
Britain	99¾	15.8	6.4	7.3	13.7

*For Canada, 1971–73 and 1971–75.

SOURCE OECD, *Historical Statistics: Economic Outlook*, Dec. 1982 two immediately preceding years) in the group of four countries with the highest rate of increase in the real-wage gap over the period 1972–75 – and, correspondingly, of course, monetary growth was less in the other three countries than in any of those four countries.

Within each of these two groups of countries, however, the ranking in terms of the real-wage gap was not the same as that for monetary growth. The respective rises in the two budgetary variables do, however, help to explain these differences of ranking within each group.

Taking first the group of four countries – Japan, Britain, France and Italy – with the largest real-wage gap over the period, we find that Italy had the fastest monetary growth, but the lowest rise in real wage rates. But the very low rate of increase over the preceding decade, or over the years of the early 1970s, in the ratio of government current receipts to GDP in Italy (the lowest of the seven) is consistent with the view that, for any given monetary growth rate, money wage increases may be expected to be lower if taxes are not rising sharply. Similarly, the fact that the real-wage gap over this period was greater for Britain than for France can be reasonably attributed to both the faster monetary growth in Britain and the larger increases in total government outlays and receipts, taken together (relative to GDP) in Britain. Moreover, the relative positions of France and Japan within this group may be related to the relative changes in the settings of their policy indicators. Although monetary growth in Japan was far faster than in France, it was not very much faster if allowance is made for the much higher rate of real economic growth in Japan; but France had much smaller increases over this period in both budgetary ratios than did Japan (and also if the comparison is taken back over a slightly longer period of years, to the later 1960s). Those relatively greater rises in the budgetary ratios in Japan may therefore help to explain why the wage gap in Japan was appreciably greater than that in France (even though Japan had an only slightly greater monetary growth rate relative to real GDP growth), and the actual budgetary ratios in Japan were much lower than for France.

Turning now to the group of three countries with the lowest increase in the real-wage gap over the period 1972–75, the place of the US at the bottom of this group (with the smallest real wage gap) is consistent with the US having the second lowest monetary growth (relative to real GDP growth) rate over the period covered among these three countries, coupled with virtually no rise in the ratio of government receipts to GDP over the period 1970–75, and a smaller rise in the ratio of government outlays to GDP than Germany or Canada (the other two countries in the group) since 1970.

Germany had the lowest monetary growth rate of the three in 1970–75, but a rather larger real-wage gap than Canada. But Germany had a bigger rise than Canada in the ratio to GDP of both government current receipts and total government outlays.

In every case, therefore, within each of these two groups, where the ranking of countries in terms of their relative real-wage gap is not the same as that for monetary growth (relative to real GDP growth), the relative changes in the budgetary ratios can help to explain the differences in ranking, if we accept the view that rising ratios of government receipts and outlays make it harder to restrain real wage increases (relative to productivity).

There does, in short, appear to be some relationship between high rates of monetary growth and the appearance of a real-wage gap over these years; but it is also likely, on the basis of this evidence, that the relative rate of increase in the budgetary variables, especially of government current receipts, contributed to influencing the relative extent of a real-wage gap in the different countries. In any case, *both* monetary *and* budgetary factors are required to explain the differences in ranking on the real wage gaps.

Over the longer period from 1972 to 1980–81 the greatest real-wage gaps (on the OECD measure cited above) were shown by France, Italy and Japan. Britain (the country with the largest gap in the 1972–75 period) showed the smallest gap over this longer period (the big rises in real wages in the earlier years having been reversed by the end of the period) because of the loss of the capacity of many of the less productive firms (and consequent sharp fall in productivity *per head of population* on that account). If allowance is made for this factor of higher unemployment in Britain, it appears that the real wage gap in Britain (over much the same period) actually exceeded that in the other major countries.* The US, Canada and Germany were the other countries in this group with relatively small real-wage gaps over this period.

The three countries – France, Italy and Japan – in the group that had the largest real-wage gaps over this period were also the three among the major seven that had by far the largest rises in both the budgetary ratios over the whole decade. Moreover, as Table 5.6

*See J. Sachs (1983).

shows, the extent of the rise in these ratios was roughly the same for each of these three, and the rise in their real wage gap was also somewhat similar – and clearly greater than for any of the other major countries. Of these three, Italy (with the second-largest real-wage gap) had the fastest rate of monetary growth of all the major countries; but, on the other hand, monetary growth in Japan and France was not among the three highest of the seven (when monetary growth is adjusted to allow for relative rates of growth in real GDP). Japan had a slightly smaller real-wage gap over this period than did Italy; its rate of monetary growth was less, and though its budgetary ratios were rising rather faster than those for Italy, their actual levels were a good deal lower.

In all, therefore, this evidence for these three countries suggests that the rises in the budgetary ratios were rather more important than relative monetary growth rates in terms of their relationship to ranking these countries in relation to their real-wage gaps over this period.

Within the other group of four countries, which had relatively lower real wage gaps over this period, the position of Britain at the bottom of the list cannot be explained in terms of the mix – unless allowance is made also for the effects of the much greater rise in unemployment and loss of capacity in Britain than in the other major countries. Among this group, Germany had an actual fall in real wages relative to productivity over the period 1972–81, and the fact that it had the lowest monetary growth rate may help to explain this. It is true that Germany had also the largest rise in the government outlay ratio over this period as a whole, and the rise in current government receipts in Germany was second only to that of Britain within this group, but those ratios hardly rose at all for Germany in the second half of the 1970s. The US had the second smallest real-wage gap over this period, and the lowest rises in the budgetary ratios as well as the second lowest monetary growth rate. Canada had the largest real-wage gap over this period among this group, and its monetary growth rate was second only to that of Britain (after allowing for relative growth of real GDP).

In short, therefore, over both the shorter period 1972–75 and the longer period 1972–81, there does appear to have been a discernible relationship between the extent of a real-wage gap and the setting of macroeconomic instruments. But over the shorter period it appears to have been relative monetary growth rates that were the more important influence, whereas over the longer period the large rises in the budgetary ratios in the three countries with the largest real-wage gaps seem to have had the closest association with relative performance among the seven in terms of the size of the real-wage gaps on this definition.

THE MAJOR SEVEN: YEAR-TO-YEAR CHANGES IN POLICY, 1967–82

The Appendix (p. 113) describes tests carried out on the year-to-year changes in the settings of the main macroeconomic instruments (as indicated by changes in the ratio of government current receipts and total government outlays to GDP, and monetary growth rates) over the period 1967–82 in the seven major OECD countries plus Australia. The purpose of these tests is to see whether the rate of inflation in any given year (as indicated by the rise in the Consumer Price Index) tends to be greater when that year is preceded by relatively large increases in the ratios of government outlays and current receipts to GDP, and in real interest rates or monetary growth (that is, M1 plus quasi-money), or in real interest rates over the two immediately preceding years. (Tests were also carried out over a total of *four* preceding years.

As the very large changes in the price of oil in certain years from 1973 onwards appeared likely to have had important effects on the change in the CPI in a number of years during the 1970s, this variable was also included in the tests, and was found to have a significant association with the change in the CPI in the same year as the change in oil prices. The association between the rate of inflation and the preceding changes in the macroeconomic policy indicators is thus measured after taking into account the apparent effect of the oil price changes.

In addition, as each individual country presumably has distinctive characteristics that make it different from the average for the group, allowance is also made for this. For example, some countries may be able to withstand a sharper increase in tax rates than others without such a large effect on the CPI – partly according to whether the tax changes are widely perceived as being equitable; and some countries may have a successful and well established prices and incomes policy, which may enable them to minimise the inflationary effects of certain macroeconomic policy changes. As the present aim is to ascertain what can be learned from the experience of the whole group about how the price level will respond to preceding changes in the mix, after allowing for any systematic differences among the countries, a factor was included in the tests to allow for these national differences (in the shape of a 'dummy variable' for each country).

These seven countries are all large enough for there to be a strong presumption that the setting of their macroeconomic instruments will have an appreciable effect within the country applying the policy in question. At the same time, they are all, to varying degrees, susceptible to outside influences of one sort or another – including the setting of macroeconomic policy in other countries. To that extent, the macroeconomic outcome in any one of them could be expected to be less dominated by the setting of its own macroeconomic policy measures than one could expect of the relatively much less 'open' economy of the OECD as a whole, or (for all of them apart from the US) more than for any of the constituent sub-divisions of it discussed in Chapter 4. (The US alone among individual countries was treated as a sub-division of the OECD in that chapter, as it is probably less 'open', in the relevant sense, than are some of the groups of countries included in the analysis.)

In the tests reported in the Appendix here for the major seven, the experience of each of these countries carries the same weight. This means that the conclusions are not dominated by the experience of the US, despite its larger economic size compared with the others.

The tests assess the extent of the association between the rate of inflation in each country in a given year and the changes in the setting of the mix during the two preceding years. For comparison, the relationship of inflation in each year to the change in monetary growth rates (alone), was also tested (the change in the most recent year proving not to have a significant association with the rise in the CPI in the year that is being explained). There proved to be a significant association between inflation and monetary growth (alone) two years previously, but it was nothing like as strong as that between the rate of inflation and the three indicators of the mix – monetary growth rates, rises in tax rates and government outlays ratios – taken together.

The relationship between the rate of inflation in a particular year and the rise in the ratio of government current receipts to GDP in the most recent year is not markedly stronger (and in some cases it is actually weaker) than its relationship to tax rises in the year before that. The relationship between tax rises and inflation cannot, therefore, on this evidence be attributed merely to any tendency there may be for tax receipts to rise in the current year as a result of a higher rate of inflation in the current year. (For, obviously, a high rate of inflation in the current year could not have increased tax receipts a year ago.) As one could reasonably have expected tax rises to have had a significant effect on the price level up to at least two years later, this significant relationship of the rate of inflation to tax changes in *both* of the two preceding years is what one could reasonably have expected.

Much the same may be said of the relationship between inflation and rises in government outlays; more or less equal weight appears to attach to the rise in the ratio of government outlays to GDP over each of the two preceding years in contributing to the association with the rate of inflation in a given year. Moreover, changes in real interest rates over each of those two preceding years appear to have had a more or less equal weight in the relationship between (falling) real interest rates and (rising) rates of inflation.

These tests therefore suggest that all these indicators of the mix have a significant association with the rate of inflation up to at least two years after the change in the setting of these macroeconomic instruments, and in the directions suggested by the a priori reasoning outlined in Chapter 2. Especially as these tests allow for any systematic differences among the countries, and also allow for the apparent effect of changes in the real price of oil, they are in fact much more impressive evidence of the association between the mix and the rate of inflation in a particular year than the much simpler statistical comparisons provided in the tables in this and the two preceding chapters (although the less econometrically minded reader may find it easier to appreciate the simpler comparisons provided in those tables).

It should be emphasised, however, that no such tests can 'prove' whether the macroeconomic mix affects the price level. All they can show is that the evidence is consistent with the hypothesis – in this case that the setting of the macroeconomic instruments, as indicated by changes in the budgetary ratios and in monetary growth or real interest rates over the two preceding years is likely to influence the rise in the CPI in any given year, and that they do so in the directions that could have been expected in the light of the a priori analysis summarised in Chapter 2 (and more fully in the earlier books).

By the same token, therefore, they provide no support for the sort of policies that involve tolerating high levels of unemployment in the hope that it will reduce inflation; because, even if a rise in unemployment does tend to have that effect with a given macroeconomic policy mix, it is clearly indefensible to tolerate high unemployment for this purpose if a change in the mix (at a given level of unemployment) would have the same effect on inflation over the period in question. In some of the formulations of the tests unemployment did not even have a significant relationship to inflation once account was taken of the setting of macroeconomic instruments.

The evidence of these tests is therefore clear that a tightening of monetary policy – either in the form of a rise in real interest rates or a slowing down of monetary growth – tended to be followed within a two-year period by some reduction in the rise in the CPI; and that, similarly, a rise in the ratio of government outlays or current receipts to GDP tended to be followed by correspondingly greater rises in the CPI. By the same token, a rise in the real rate of interest, or a slowing down of monetary growth, or a reduction in the rise in either of the budgetary ratios, tended to be followed by a reduction in the rise in the CPI within a two-year period.

Policies taking account of these results should therefore be directed at reducing stagflation by some combination of tight monetary policy, and slower rises in both government current receipts and many types of government outlays, coupled with an overall setting of policy that would tend to reduce unemployment.

Indeed, the results of the tests are very much more supportive of such policies than the minimum that would be required to justify such a mix. For the tests consistently showed that a tax cut (taken alone, and with a given setting of monetary policy) tends to *reduce* the annual rate of inflation; whereas all that would really have been required was that if a tax cut had tended to increase the rate of inflation it should have done so to a smaller extent than an easing of monetary policy or a rise in government outlays having the same effect in reducing unemployment. *If* the tests had indicated that tax cuts tended to *increase* inflation it would thus have been necessary to complement them by other tests of the relative effect of tax cuts and higher government outlays or easier monetary policy in stimulating employment or output. But, as it is, it can be said that if a government uses a tax cut to try to reduce unemployment, it could reasonably expect to reduce inflation as well (provided, of course, that it does not permit also a considerable monetary expansion).

6 Conclusions for Policy

This chapter summarises the macroeconomic conclusions of the foregoing chapters, and then sets their policy implications against the context of economic policy generally.

Consideration is given to the question whether the less inflationary mixes might ever all have such adverse effects on the allocation of resources that it could even be worth tolerating temporarily high unemployment rather than employing one of the anti-inflationary mixes. Although such a situation might conceivably arise at near to full employment, it seems virtually certain that when there are high levels of macroeconomic unemployment there will be anti-inflationary mixes that will tend to reduce the rate of inflation over the period in question without any risk that they may have adverse resource allocation effects sufficient to outweigh their macroeconomic benefits. At the same time, it is possible to conceive of particular anti-inflationary mixes that might have seriously adverse resource allocation effects, and a government would naturally have to weigh these possible effects before choosing an appropriate mix.

The main arguments of this book have been as follows:

(1) The problem of stagflation, which surfaced in the later 1960s, became much worse in the later 1970s and early 1980s. The attempt to deal with the inflation by accepting high and rising levels of unemployment left the problem essentially unresolved, as governments remained reluctant to adopt policies that would restore full employment – in the expectation that to do so would increase inflation again to unacceptable rates.

(2) Part of the problem was itself the result of the combinations of taxation, government outlays and monetary policy employed from the later 1960s onwards, when there was a sharp rise in the ratios to GDP of government receipts and outlays; and from the early 1970s onwards monetary policy, as indicated by the rate of growth of monetary aggregates (relative to the growth of real output) and by real interest rates (especially after tax), also

moved in a direction that could have been expected to increase the upward pressure on the price level at any given level of unemployment. Groups of countries that had especially rapid monetary growth and large rises in their budgetary ratios tended to have higher rates of inflation. But there is no such evidence of any clear relationship between unemployment and relative rates of inflation, or between budget deficits and inflation.

(3) An important part of the solution must therefore lie in choosing more appropriate combinations of macroeconomic measures. Indeed, provided that there is even one macroeconomic stimulus that is less inflationary than some other there is in principle a combination of the two that will exert a downward pressure on the price level comparable to that which governments are presumably hoping to achieve by their current policies of temporarily high unemployment. It is therefore not justifiable to tolerate the high unemployment if a change of the mix – coupled with appropriately more expansionary policies – can reduce the rise in the price level without having to accept the high unemployment.

(4) A change in the mix towards a lower ratio to GDP of government receipts and of the more inflationary forms of government outlay, coupled with a reasonably tight monetary policy, needs to be coupled with a sufficiently expansionary overall policy to restore full employment. The greater the extent to which higher levels of activity are thought likely to increase inflation, the greater the change of mix (in an appropriate direction) that would need to accompany the recovery.

(5) In certain respects, however, the high levels of unemployment (and the associated below-capacity operation of firms) may have been tending to increase the upward pressure on the price level; and, to that extent, recovery could be accompanied by a reduction in unit costs (which would tend to have some downward impact on prices). At the level of the firm, operating below capacity raises unit costs, and to that extent the incentive for manufacturers to charge higher prices. Moreover, the financing of the government sector at a time when the economy is operating well below capacity necessitates governments raising their charges and tax rates (per unit of service provided, and per unit of output produced in the economy), in order to finance the overhead costs of government, including those government outlays (such as defence and most of the public service) that do not vary much, if at all, with the level of economic activity.

MACROECONOMIC MEASURES TO STOP STAGFLATION

An important part of the changes in policy that are required to solve the problem of stagflation is a reversal of the almost universal tendency for tax receipts to rise as a proportion of GDP. It is also necessary to reduce the tendency for certain of the more inflationary forms of government outlay – notably defence spending and transfer payments – to rise in relation to total output. A recovery of real output sufficient to reduce unemployment would, however, tend to reduce some forms of government outlay, such as unemployment benefit payments, and would to that extent make it easier to maintain (without serious cost inflation) any given outlay on other transfers or on defence (or on other items that do not directly add to the output of marketable goods and services). Indeed, a recovery of real output towards its potential might make it possible to have levels of government outlay on goods and services at least as high as the present ones in absolute terms even if they were lower in relation to total output: trying to hold down government outlays whilst also holding down activity may well *raise* the ratio of government outlays to GDP.

The worst forms of stimulus are those that are most widely asked for by businessmen and journalists, and generally favoured by politicians – especially those forms that operate through easier monetary policies with the aim of reducing interest rates. For such measures certainly increase the upward pressure on prices at any given level of unemployment (by comparison with tax cuts, and some forms of government outlay, having the same effect on employment). Indeed, easier monetary policies may well increase not only inflation but also interest rates, once the higher rates of inflation have had time to affect interest rates. Paradoxically, therefore, it is a mix with *tight* monetary policies that may well do most, at least in the medium to long run, to hold *down* nominal interest rates at any given level of employment.

Tax cuts tend to reduce cost-inflation. They can also be normally expected to increase employment even if they are wholly financed by borrowing from the non-bank public. But if (by some extraordinary chance) the net effect of such an operation were *not* to produce a stimulus to employment tax cuts would then have the overwhelming advantage for dealing with stagflation that they could (in this purely hypothetical situation) be proceeded with as far as would be necessary in order to eliminate inflation – for tax cuts could in those circumstances have no demand-inflationary effects, so that (as the taxes that were reduced would have had some cost-increasing effects) tax cuts could only reduce inflation. At the same time, any necessary stimulus could then (in this hypothetical case) be given by monetary means.

In fact, of course, tax cuts must normally be expected to increase employment by adding to effective demand; and to that extent may have some demand–inflationary effects that will need to be offset by a sufficiently tight monetary policy (to prevent the tax cuts from leading to too rapid an increase in monetary aggregates), or else by a reduction of the share of government outlays to total output (or, of course, by some combination of the two). But the less the stimulus to activity resulting from a given tax cut (and the greater the reduction in costs and other prices resulting from it) the less would be any tightening of monetary policy (or cuts in the ratio to GDP of government outlays) that would be necessary to hold employment at any given level in the face of the tax cuts. Indeed, when tax rates are initially high a stimulus that is accompanied by reductions in inflation is perfectly possible. The contrary assumption is usually made largely because in the past a stimulus has usually been given by an inflationary mix of (mainly) easy money and rises in government outlays, rather than by way of tax cuts.

It is not helpful simply to urge governments to reduce budget deficits. For if they do so by raising tax rates, they will certainly make the problem of stagflation worse. In any event, their efforts to reduce budget deficits are likely to reduce employment still more, and this may even increase their budget deficits still further. But, whether or not that happens, cutting the budget deficit by tax increases alone will both raise unemployment and make cost-inflation worse. On the other hand, the same reduction in the budget deficit brought about by reducing the more inflationary forms of government outlay could at least reduce the upward pressure on the price level at any given level of employment.

It would be more appropriate from a macroeconomic point of view, therefore, to urge governments to reduce their excessive real (cyclically adjusted) budget surpluses, or raise their inadequate real budget deficits, but to do so mainly (or solely) by tax cuts, whilst pursuing monetary policies, that would ensure, in combination with the tax cuts, that the monetary aggregates did not rise excessively; but with an overall setting of budgetary and monetary policies such as to ensure that that full employment is restored progressively. It is by no means certain that, even if reductions in budget deficits were effected mainly by curtailing the more inflationary forms of government outlay, this would help to solve the problem; for, taken alone, such a policy may well increase unemployment, even if it reduces the upward pressure on the price level at any given level of unemployment. Moreover, if the deflationary effects of such a policy were offset by an easing of monetary policy – which is usually the aim of the advocates of such a mix – this may well be a more inflationary way than any other of preventing unemployment from rising any further (even if it succeeds in reducing unemployment). A lower ratio of government outlays to GDP may thus necessitate a *larger* budget deficit in order to establish a given (or lower) level of unemployment.

It is therefore extremely dangerous to follow the widespread practice of suggesting that a country should 'reduce the budget deficit'; for whereas some forms of budget deficit reduction may help to reduce the risk of stagflation continuing, other ways of achieving the same reduction in the budget deficit will certainly make matters worse. If one is advocating a change in the budget deficit or surplus, one should therefore spell out the form that that change should take.

If the real case being argued is for reductions in those forms of government outlay that are felt to be a waste of resources, this case should be stated explicitly. If, on the other hand, what is being argued is that tax rates should be increased, it should be acknowledged that this will in all likelihood increase the upward pressure on the price level at any given level of employment (and with a given monetary growth rate).

There are measures that can helpfully be undertaken in a period of stagflation that will incidentally tend to reduce the budget deficit (at any given level of employment). An appropriate curtailment of any unnecessary and wasteful forms of government outlays should be undertaken in any event; and social security payments, as well as the various forms of income-support policies, should be confined to those in need, instead of (as now) being spread across many income groups in the hope of buying votes. Reductions in these forms of outlay (as a ratio of total output) are likely to make it easier to reduce stagflation, and will incidentally tend to reduce the budget deficit; but they should be favoured for the contribution that such cuts will make to restoring full employment without inflation – and not *because* they are likely to reduce the budget deficit. If accompanied by appropriate tax cuts, reductions in such outlays could be a helpful element in a policy tending to raise employment; and if the price-reducing effects of these tax and outlay cuts were large, a sufficient real stimulus *might* be provided with a constant, or even falling, budget deficit.

TARGETS AND THE MIX

Just as policies directed towards a particular budget deficit target are dangerous – as being just as likely to make stagflation worse as to reduce it – so monetary targets are dangerous for the same sort of reasons. A reduction in monetary growth of a given amount may be helpful so far as it is achieved with a price-reducing mix (mainly restraints in the more inflationary forms of government outlays or sales of bonds to the non-bank public), but could be harmful so far as it was achieved mainly by way of relatively high tax rates. If policy-makers were to be justified in pursuing particular figures for targets like the budget outturn ('deficit') or the growth of a particular monetary aggregate (as such), it would be necessary for them to establish a strong presumption that a given budget deficit or surplus, or a given growth of a particular monetary aggregate, would have the same effect on the price level for a given effect on employment *irrespective of the combination of tax rates, government outlays, and monetary policy* (sale of government securities to the non-bank public) *by means of which it was achieved*. The evidence outlined in earlier chapters of this book suggests that no such presumption could reasonably be based on the experience of the OECD countries between the later 1960s and the early 1980s. Indeed, that evidence is consistent with the view that tax rises make it harder to hold down the price level, with any given monetary growth rate, and with any given level of government outlays; and that increases in some forms of government outlays (at least) as a ratio of GDP make it similarly hard to hold down the price level. Policies that result in a rise in the ratio of government revenue to GDP, and of many types of government outlays to GDP, thus make it harder to prevent stagflation. By the same token, if governments are willing to keep monetary policy tight, but to restrain the rise in both the ratio of tax receipts to GDP and that of the more inflationary forms of government outlay to GDP, they can reduce the upward pressure on the price level at any given level of employment; and it is to that extent unjustifiable to tolerate a higher level of unemployment than would otherwise have been felt necessary in order to attempt thereby to hold down the price level.

Certainly, the evidence considered in earlier chapters of the present book is that success in holding down the budget deficit (or the increase in it) has no clear relationship to success in holding down inflation; whereas the extent to which the budgetary ratios have increased does have a clear relationship to rates of inflation. This is exactly what one would expect if one way of reducing a budget deficit – cuts in the ratio to GDP of the more inflationary forms of government outlay – tends to *reduce* the upward pressures on the price level at any given level of employment, whereas other ways of effecting the same reduction in the budget deficit – tax increases – add to the upward pressure on prices at a given level of employment. So far as that is true, therefore, one could not expect the level of the budget deficit itself, or changes in it, to have any discernible relationship to the rate of inflation observed during a period when changes in these ratios were occurring.

Moreover, the evidence suggests that the level of unemployment in itself clearly has no relationship to success in checking inflation (apart, that is, from the particular combination of measures with which any given level of employment is established). Again, this is what one could expect if some measures that tend to increase unemployment are cost-inflationary (in one way or another), whereas others are not.

If governments are influenced by such intermediate variables as the budget deficit or monetary growth, it is thus important that they look also at indicators of both sides of the budget, as well as indicators of the setting of monetary policy, and ensure that the combination of the various macroeconomic instruments with which they achieve a given monetary growth will be one that is likely to have the most helpful effect in restraining inflation without raising unemployment.

It may well be possible to obtain better indicators of the settings of the various macroeconomic instruments than those used generally in this book; for the indicators used here have been ones that are affected not only by policy decisions but (like the budget deficit) also by events in the economy that are not the result of policy changes. Ideally, one would like some form of cyclically adjusted indicators for all these instruments of macroeconomic policy.

POLICY AND WAGE RATES

If one of the problems of industrialised countries is that, in some of them at least, real wages have been increased to levels that cannot be sustained (given present levels of productivity) without high unemployment, the possibility that the mix may affect real wage rates (as some evidence given in Chapter 5 suggests) may commend appropriate variations in the mix to those who emphasise real wages as an important influence on employment.

But, irrespective of the weight that one assigns to those considerations, a mix that holds down the rate of increase in *money* wage rates is likely to be helpful in improving the macroeconomic situation (in the sense of reducing the upward pressure on the price level at any given level of employment). It may or may not also reduce *real* wages as a cost; for one can never know whether prices in the period when the wages are being paid will be brought down as much (or more) than the reduction in money wage increases that may result from a change of mix. One cannot, in other words, in practice operate on *real* wage rates, but only (at best) on *money* wage rates. (Very often, however, the phrase 'a reduction in real wage rates' is used to describe a rise in money wage rates in a given period that is slower than the rise in consumer prices that has occurred *in the preceding period*; but this need not necessarily lead to any reduction in real wage costs during the period when the wages are being paid.)

It is therefore likely to be useful to adopt policies that will reduce the rate of increase in money incomes, including money wage rates, as well as in the taxes paid by businesses, in periods when stagflation is a problem, provided that policies are directed also at ensuring that if this does not by itself lead to the desired fall in unemployment other measures will be adopted to have that effect. No one can know for certain how far excessive real wage costs (including taxes on employment) are the reason for high unemployment; the best policy is thus at any rate to reduce those costs in nominal terms, but to adopt appropriate policies to ensure that full employment will be restored by other means so far as that proves necessary when wage increases are slowed down and tax rates cut.

MACROECONOMIC MIXES AND RESOURCE ALLOCATION POLICY

We have so far in this chapter discussed the choice of macroeconomic policies from the viewpoint of minimising the upward pressure on the price level at a given level of activity – rather than using temporarily high levels of unemployment with the aim (or in the hope) of thereby restraining inflation.

In the present section we consider whether there may ever, in principle, be situations where a price-reducing mix might justifiably not be chosen because it had certain unfavourable effects on the allocation of resources that might exceed its helpful macroeconomic effects.

It appears that vague misgivings on this score must underlie the general reluctance of governments to choose less inflationary mixes (and correspondingly more expansionary policies). But it must be observed that in order to defend high-unemployment policies it would be necessary to establish that every possible change of mix that might reduce the rate of inflation would have adverse welfare effects in excess of those welfare gains to be achieved by operating the economy nearer to full employment with one of the anti-inflationary mixes.

If the argument were that, even in the short run, adverse resource allocation effects might result, and that these might negate the price-reducing effects of the change of mix, then these considerations should be taken into account when deciding the relative effects on inflation of alternative ways of affecting employment. We shall therefore be concerned in what follows, first, with possible longer-run effects, which may influence future macroeconomic success; and, secondly, with other possible effects on the economic welfare of present and future generations that might result from the adoption of some anti-inflationary mixes. Any adverse effects on the country's welfare that may result (for example) from reducing the ratio to GDP of certain price-increasing forms of government outlay (such as defence spending) must be given their due weight in formulating macroeconomic policy.

A SOUND MIX, PROTECTIONISM AND RESISTANCE TO CHANGE

But it must be borne in mind, as a background to all the ensuing discussion, that any mix that reduces the upward pressure on the price level, and to that extent makes a government readier to operate the economy nearer to full employment (rather than use temporarily high unemployment as the means of trying to restrain inflation), carries a certain big resource allocation advantage over other macroeconomic policies.

For high levels of unemployment do severe damage to the effectiveness with which the world uses its resources, by encouraging protectionism in all its forms. It is very difficult to resist political pressures for maintaining or increasing assistance to economically weak or inefficient firms and industries when unemployment is high and when profitability generally is low. In addition to all the economic costs of failing to employ resources fully, therefore, there is also this economic cost of the misallocation of those resources that are employed. As different countries react against each others' policies by various types of limitations on imports of particular products, this cost becomes cumulative and mutually re-inforcing on a global scale.

Furthermore, employees are reluctant to tolerate and cooperate in the introduction of new methods when there are high general levels of unemployment. A precondition for making proper use of the available techniques is to adopt macroeconomic policies that ensure there are jobs for all – but not necessarily in the work on which they are employed at present.

CURRENT POLICIES CONTRASTED WITH SWITCHES OF THE MIX

If there is to be any justification for the macroeconomic policies of recent years it has to be that by tolerating temporarily very high levels of unemployment the governments concerned hope to reduce the rate of inflation permanently, so that they can subsequently restore full employment with only a tolerable rate of inflation; and that there is no way of achieving the same macroeconomic ends without the loss of output and employment over the interim period. It would be necessary also, even in that case, in order to justify policies involving high unemployment, to make the judgment that the social costs of tolerating the high unemployment and loss of output would be outweighed by the welfare gains that would eventually be derived from having reduced inflation by this means. If, however, the loss of ourput was very large, and had to be very long sustained – and, still more so, if it had to be accepted that full employment would never be restored (or not for a very long time) – the case for such policies would clearly be correspondingly weaker.

But, for the present discussion, we shall assume that current policies do provide a viable alternative to changes of the mix as a means of reducing inflation over the period in question. We shall further assume (without accepting that the assumption is realistic) that these policies, re-inforced if necessary, by subsequent reflationary measures, will make it possible to restore full employment (on whatever definition is considered appropriate). The comparison will therefore be between such a policy and the use of some form of change of mix to achieve the same effect on inflation over the interim period, but without the loss of output and employment opportunities.

THE MIX AND PRODUCTIVE INVESTMENT

A mix of tight monetary policy coupled with tax cuts is often criticised on the grounds that it will allegedly tend to reduce investment. This will not, however, necessarily be the effect of such a mix, and, even if it is, that is not a sufficient ground upon which to oppose such a mix, especially if the alternative is to use temporarily high levels of unemployment in order to attempt to hold down inflation.

In the first place, a shift toward tighter monetary policy and general tax cuts will not necessarily reduce 'investment' – by which is meant those forms of outlay that are influenced by the level of interest rates. For a change of mix towards higher post-tax interest rates (without pre-tax interest rates needing to rise as much – or even at all) may permit, at any given price level, an increase in output sufficient to satisfy the higher demand for consumption goods and services without investment falling. Moreover, so far as the higher interest rates increase saving, the danger to investment will be less.* Moreover, the types of 'investment' that are discouraged may be those that are normally thought of as 'consumption' – spending on housing and consumer durables – rather than on those forms of productive material investment that help to determine future productivity growth, and which it is usually desired to encourage. With a given propensity to save, or a given level of total savings at the higher level of activity, an appropriate combination of taxes and subsidies may be employed to ensure that the level of productive investment is

*The conditions under which such a shift of mix will not reduce the level of investment have been examined by I. M. McDonald (1984). He there suggests that there is no general presumption that investment will fall rather than rise as a result of such policies.

not unduly reduced (if at all) by the change of mix. Total available output will be greater – at least in the short run – if a less inflationary mix is employed (rather than temporarily higher unemployment) to restrain inflation; an appropriate structure of taxes and subsidies should be able to ensure that part or all of that extra output is channelled towards making good any reduction there might be in those forms of productive material investment that it is desired to safeguard in the interests of future prosperity. But so far as the main influence on investment is likely to be the restoration of a higher level of activity, a more appropriate mix coupled with a more expansionary policy is at least as likely to increase productive investment as to reduce it.

In any case, although it may be a reasonable simplification to assume that investment is initially at the ideal ratio to total output (in order to focus on short-run macroeconomic issues), it may in fact be at, below or above that level. The more one is concerned with the welfare of the present generation, the less one may be inclined to try to raise that ratio, and the readier to tolerate a fall in it. Moreover, even if one wants to raise it, the alternative is available of reducing the more inflationary forms of government outlay, and of releasing resources to productive investment through that route, rather than by keeping tax rates higher than would otherwise have been chosen. Any welfare losses from such cuts in government outlays would have to be set against the benefits of the consequently higher level of productive investment.

Furthermore, even if the level of productive material investment were reduced by the change of mix accompanied by measures to reduce the level of unemployment, the fuller use of the available work force made possible by that policy will increase the stock of human capital, as more people will (as a result of such policies) have had work experience that may be expected to enable them to make a greater contribution to output in future than if they had remained unemployed. This favourable effect on the stock of human capital would have to be set against any reduction there might be in the stock of material capital.

Finally in this context, even if the stock of human and material capital together were reduced by the policies (of tax cuts and tight monetary policy) below what they would otherwise have been, and below what would have been desired in the long run (which seems an unlikely situation), there could still reasonably be expected to be a social gain to be derived from adopting a policy that involved lower unemployment and a change of mix (rather than relatively high unemployment) to check inflation. For the more expansionary policy coupled with the change of mix would avoid the human suffering that would result from the temporarily high level of unemployment. Provided that we are comparing two policies that would leave the economy at the same eventual level of unemployment and inflation, common sense would suggest that the one with lower unemployment in the interim would be socially preferable. Certainly, that presumption could be overthrown only if there were strong reasons to believe that the stock of human plus material capital would be very much *lower* as a result of the more expansionary policies (whereas the presumption ought in fact to be that the total capital stock would be larger under such policies).

If the net result were in fact to reduce long-run productivity growth below what it would otherwise have been, however, this would make it correspondingly harder to hold down inflation in future. Even if that were not the result, one would wish to take due account of whatever effect – favourable or unfavourable – on the welfare of posterity might result from any given macroeconomic policy. But these arguments do not, on any commonsense view, upset the general presumption that, starting from high levels of unemployment, the best thing we can do for posterity is to stop stagflation as quickly as possible by reducing unemployment by a price-reducing mix of measures. If the waste of resources resulting from policies that tolerate high unemployment, including the adverse resource allocation effects that these have through protectionism and resistance of employees to technical progress, can thereby be avoided, posterity will inherit a correspondingly larger stock of capital on that account. It would require a very sharp (and highly unlikely) reduction in the stock of human and material capital (taken together) to result from a change of mix (plus a more expansionary policy) for it to be possible to conclude that posterity would benefit by a continuation of very high levels of unemployment. Nevertheless, as the economy recovers nearer to full employment the possibilities of further gain to be derived from operating at nearer to full employment will inevitably diminish, so that it is possible that the least inflationary mixes – involving tax cuts and relatively high real rates of interest – might in some circumstances then have adverse resource allocation effects that would justify the choice of some other mix (less likely to hold down the price level, perhaps, but having less adverse effects on the allocation of resources).

THE MIX AND FUTURE TAX RATES

Those mixes that involve a higher level of the budget deficit and net additions to the national debt during the period in which they are being applied, may be thought likely to result in higher levels of taxation in future; and if this is so one may argue that that would increase the macroeconomic problems of the future, so far as taxes may then have cost-increasing effects at that future time.

But this is not likely, in principle, to be a sound reason for failing to adopt a price-reducing mix. In the first place, even if tax rates in future have to be higher as a result of adopting such a mix, one might either elect to give less weight to the problems of posterity, or argue that there is no reason why their macroeconomic problems should be be the same as ours. In any case, if posterity believes that the increase of its tax rates will bring it net social costs, it would have to consider the alternative of lower ratios of the more inflationary forms of government outlay to GDP – and that might *reduce* the upward pressure on the price level. Nevertheless, that policy would bring its own form of social costs for posterity.

The probability is, however, that if we adopt a mix that enables us to operate the economy nearer to full employment in the near future, this will enable us to bequeath to posterity a larger stock of human and material capital than if we continued to try to hold down inflation by operating the economy at well below full employment. This larger stock of capital would enable posterity to finance any given level of interest payments with lower tax rates than if the tax base had been smaller.

If, however, we take the view that, despite those considerations, we do not wish to make the addition to the national debt that would result from the bond sales and tax cuts in question, we could choose to adopt a price-reducing mix that would not add to the national debt, or would do so to a much smaller extent (an extent that is likely to be offset by the larger stock of human and material capital we would consequently be able to bequeath to posterity). An extreme form of such a mix would be a reduction in the ratio to GDP of one of the more inflationary forms of government outlay – transfer payments – together with an equal reduction in the ratio of tax revenue to GDP. The consequent downward pressure on the price level (and associated rise in real money balances) at a given level of disposable income would be a form of stimulus operating purely through price reductions.

Indeed, so far as the consequent fall in unemployment reduced unemployment benefit payments, such a stimulus might even be consistent with the budget moving somewhat in the direction of surplus. Similarly, so far as such a change of mix stimulated economic activity, it would tend to increase tax revenue with any given set of nominal tax rates; so that this factor, too, would tend to reduce the actual budget deficits. Combinations of stimulus with changes of mix are thus in principle available that need not increase the level of national debt bequeathed to posterity. But one can readily conceive of policies that would go further towards reducing tax rates, and increasing the national debt, but which would still leave posterity better off, as a result of the larger stock of human capital it had inherited as a result of our more appropriate macroeconomic policies (even if material capital were lower, and even if there involved larger realised budget deficits than would have resulted from more inflationary mixes of higher tax rates and easier monetary policies).

REDUCING GOVERNMENT OUTLAY RATIOS

So long as there are any forms of government outlay that could be reduced as a ratio of GDP with consequent downward pressure on the price level (at a given level of employment) there is likely to be a macroeconomic case for making such an adjustment (so long as governments continue to be concerned about unduly high levels of both unemployment and inflation).

It is true that, in formulating macroeconomic analysis, one might reasonably make the assumption that if certain forms of government outlay are excessive they ought *in any event* to be reduced, so that – however unrealistic that might be as an assumption about current policies in the real world – one can focus on macroeconomic considerations.

But if there are welfare gains to be obtained from operating the economy at nearer to full employment, provided that one uses a change of mix to exert the downward effect on the price level that one would otherwise hope to achieve by the temporarily high unemployment, one might rationally accept any welfare losses that might result from reducing somewhat the level of the more inflationary forms of government outlays below the ratio to GDP that would have been ideal if employment had been unalterably fixed at its previous level. Some reduction in those ratios would be worth accepting up to the point at which the social welfare costs from doing so were as great as the welfare gains to be derived from avoiding the unemployment that would have been the alternative means of trying to hold down inflation over the period in question. In any event, with a lower level of unemployment, one price-increasing form of government outlay will naturally be lower than under the policies of tolerating temporarily high unemployment; for, with lower levels of unemployment, total payments of unemployment benefits, and also many other social security outlays, as well as payments for early retirement, will be lower – without this involving any welfare loss.

Moreover, even a lower ratio of certain inflationary forms of government outlay to GDP – defence spending, for example – might be as high in real terms under the policy of using a change of mix, (rather than temporarily high unemployment) with the aim of trying to restrain inflation. For the country's total output would be greater, so that the overhead cost of the defence bill would represent correspondingly less per head of population, or per unit of output, than if the ratio of defence spending to GDP were higher. (In any case, it might well be that a lower real defence outlay would be appropriate if the country's total output – and to that extent its general economic strength – were higher, as it would be under the policy of using the mix instead of high unemployment to restrain inflation.)

The foregoing discussion amounts to saying that if the prevailing current policies involve tolerating high unemployment, but with levels of government outlay that are believed to be – at that level of unemployment – the ideal ratio to total output, one might nevertheless justifiably change the mix in the direction of reducing those ratios, whilst operating the economy at a higher level of output. For this would bring the welfare gain resulting from the lower unemployment (and the associated favourable resource allocation effects); and it would do so in a way that did not increase the national debt as much as would the alternative of relying on tax cuts and bond sales alone.

Ideally, the policy should be taken to the point where the welfare benefits to be derived by operating the economy at nearer to full employment without inflation, by way of the change of mix, just offset any welfare losses that are expected to result from reducing the ratio to GDP of certain government outlays, or from cutting tax rates and selling rather more government bonds to the non-bank public. In other words, the ratio to total output of certain of the more inflationary forms of government outlay that would have been ideal apart from macroeconomic considerations may be far from ideal when one introduces also the consideration that if those ratios are reduced, temporarily high unemployment may be avoided.

THE USE OF THE MIX COMPARED WITH OTHER WAYS OF INFLUENCING MONEY INCOMES

There might be no need to use variations in the mix to avoid excessive inflation at any given level of employment if some form of incomes policy were capable of exerting complete control over the general level of wage rates and other incomes. Or if it proved possible to reform the institutions of the labour market in such a way that changes in money wage rates reflected only changes in the supply and demand for particular types of labour, and if this led to full employment with a given, steady, growth of nominal GDP, it might be possible to reserve the use of variations in the macroeconomic mix solely for affecting the allocation of resources and the distribution of income.*

But the only circumstances in which it would not be defensible to make at least some use of the mix to achieve macroeconomic ends would be if the direct influence of policy over money wage rates, and indirectly over all money incomes, were so complete as to ensure the achieving of full employment without inflation by this means. Even in that case, however, if there were any costs involved in reforming labour market institutions in such a way as to have that result, there would still be a case for using variations in the mix, up to the point at which any costs involved in doing so equalled those of applying the alternative policy.

It is, however, unrealistic to assume that either prices and incomes policies or reforms of the labour market could alone achieve such macroeconomic aims as their proponents suggest for them without being supported by combinations of macroeconomic instruments that would minimise inflation at any given level of employment. The only realistic approach is therefore to make whatever use one can of *all*

* The use of variations in money wage rates with a view to maximising employment in any given occupation is suggested by Meade and Vines – the 'new Keynesian' approach, as they call it, in contrast with what they call the 'old Keynesian' approach of using wages policy to minimise the rate of increase in money incomes. See Meade (1982); and Vines, Maciejowski and Meade (1983).

the available measures. In particular, *without* a sound macroeconomic mix no other policies are likely to succeed in minimising inflation and unemployment, whereas *with* a sound mix any other measures have a better chance of success.

THE MIX AND THE DEBTOR COUNTRIES

A mix of tight monetary policy coupled with tax cuts is often criticised on the grounds that it will tend to increase the financial difficulties of debtor countries. But this is not an adequate reason for refraining from such policies if they will enable the industrialised world to operate at a higher level of activity than with a mix of easier monetary policy and higher tax rates.

The debtor countries presumably stand to gain more than others if the industrialised world successfully adopts macroeconomic policy measures that reduce inflation (by means that do not involve tolerating temporarily high levels of unemployment).

For the burden of their indebtedness is obviously greater if the debtor countries cannot readily sell their exports to the industrialised world, and if the industrialised world is holding down aid programmes as a consequence of the relatively low real incomes there that are the result of recession. This point is so fundamental – and, one would have thought, so obvious – that one must suppose that those who raise this issue are (consciously or unconsciously) assuming that the mix makes no difference to the upward pressure on the price level at a given level of employment; and are thus merely comparing the relative effects on the debtor countries of two alternative mixes (one with tight money and one with relatively easy money) *at a given level of employment.*

But once one admits the possibility that a mix of tight monetary policy coupled with tax cuts will enable the industrialised countries to operate at higher levels of activity, it seems unlikely that the debtor countries would really benefit by policies in the industrialised world involving higher unemployment there, coupled with a more inflationary mix.

If, however, the judgment is made that the benefits that the debtor countries would derive from the stronger export markets (including the benefit they would derive from consequent reductions in protectionism) in the industrialised world would be less than the costs to them of the rise in real interest rates, this would merely constitute an argument for the industrialised countries to extend appropriate forms of aid, or interest adjustments, to ensure that the debtor countries did not lose by the policy. (This would not involve shielding them from more than part of the extra interest cost.) Indeed, if this were not done one could only assume that the argument was not one to which the governments of the industrialised countries really attached any weight. For if the mix of tight monetary policy and tax cuts really were the most appropriate from the viewpoint of the industrialised world it would be absurd for the industrialised countries to tolerate instead higher levels of unemployment and more inflationary mixes, rather than adopt the more enlightened macroeconomic policies – and compensate the debtor countries for any net costs to them, so far as this was held to be a desirable aim of policy.

CONCLUSIONS

Throughout most of this book the underlying assumption – a realistic one at the time of writing – has been that governments have been generally tolerating a level of unemployment temporarily higher than they would have otherwise chosen, in the hope of thereby reducing the upward pressure on the price level. So long as this is true, the substitution of a less inflationary mix for the temporarily high level of unemployment can naturally be expected to bring considerable welfare gains by way of higher output and lower unemployment.

But even in a situation where the government is *not* tolerating temporarily high unemployment in the hope of thereby restraining inflation, the adoption of a less inflationary mix can clearly bring macroeconomic benefits – so long as the government is still concerned to hold down the rate of inflation; for such a change of mix will (at the very least) reduce the upward pressure on the price level over the period when the change of mix is occurring. It can also be expected that such a change will reduce the upward pressure on prices over a longer period, as the reduction in the rise of prices (over the period of the change of mix) will normally reduce the expected, and to that extent the actual, rate of inflation over some further period.

Moreover, a once-for-all tax cut may well have continuing downward effects on money wage increases, and to that extent hold down future inflation. For a high ratio of taxes to pre-tax wages makes it more likely that any chance increase in the price level will lead wage and salary-earners to demand correspondingly larger increases in their pre-tax wage rates; and though the obverse of this would also be true when prices of goods and services fell, a high level of taxation on wage and salary-earners could still tend to increase the average rate of inflation provided that money wage rates are more flexible upwards than downwards – and, anyway, the price level seldom falls.

Furthermore, the higher are tax rates (or the more inflationary forms of government outlay) the greater the chance of macroeconomic gain from reducing the taxes (or government outlays) as a ratio of GDP.

In short, a shift to a less inflationary mix will bring macroeconomic benefits, at least in the short run, so long as governments are concerned to hold down inflation; but those benefits will clearly be greater when there is extensive unemployment (which governments fear to reduce in case it may worsen inflation) and will be correspondingly less if the economy is close to full employment.

In finally deciding its policy measures, however, a government has also to take account of any resource allocation effects of the combination of policy measures that it adopts. If a particular mix had adverse resource allocation effects that reduced economic welfare by more than the benefits from adopting a less inflationary mix, that would constitute grounds for choosing some other mix.

Generally, however, the choice of a less inflationary mix, coupled with a higher level of employment, may be expected to have *helpful* resource allocation effects, by reducing the extent of protectionist policies and the opposition of employees to the introduction of better productive methods (which is strong when unemployment is high).

Macroeconomic measures must always be considered in the light of their macroeconomic effects, together with their likely *favourable* effects on the allocation of resources; and if they have also unwanted effects on other economic objectives, those considerations must be brought into account before the final policy decisions are made. But it is certainly not a sufficient objection to the choice of one of the less inflationary mixes to cite possible adverse effects on resource allocation that may result from it.

In the preceding section we considered a number of circumstances in which there might, in principle, be a valid case for tolerating temporarily higher levels of unemployment than would otherwise have been chosen – provided that the government was able to assume that this would hold down inflation – rather than using a less inflationary mix. But even if one can establish that some of the mixes that are most likely to hold down inflation (at least in the short run) will have certain undesirable resource allocation effects in the longer run, this would not be sufficient to constitute a valid case for tolerating temporarily high unemployment in the hope of thereby restraining inflation. For it would be necessary also to establish that *every* possible inflation-reducing mix would have adverse effects on economic welfare, through its resource allocation consequences, that would exceed the benefits from adopting a less inflationary mix. The further below full employment is the economy, the less likely is it that such a situation will arise (where temporarily high unemployment could be defensible). But there are no general grounds for expecting that any adverse resource allocation effects of a change to a less inflationary mix will normally equal or exceed the benefits from adopting a more successful macroeconomic policy. Up to the point at which the macroeconomic benefits no longer exceeded any adverse resource allocation effects, it is obviously desirable to adopt a less inflationary mix. It is clearly unlikely that all possible switches towards less inflationary mixes will (at any given time) have been carried to the point where this is so.

There is a close analogy in the field of international trade theory. The usual exposition of the basis for trade between countries (and it would also be true of trade among individuals) is that trade may occur either because there are differences of comparative advantage between countries in the production of goods and services, or in their respective tastes, or both. That is, trade may occur between countries (or individuals) because of differences of taste, even if there were no differences of comparative advantage between them in the production of different goods and services. By the same token, trade would not occur if it should happen that differences of comparative advantage between countries were exactly offset by differences in their tastes.

If, therefore, one were to refrain from making a change of mix that was desirable on macroeconomic grounds merely on the basis of the view that all such switches of mix might have (equal and opposite) undesirable resource allocation effects on economic welfare, this would be analogous to making the highly unrealistic assumption that international trade would be unlikely to occur as differences of taste would exactly offset differences of comparative advantage in production.

A switch of mix would therefore always be desirable up to the point at which the benefits from its contribution to macroeconomic success just equalled any net adverse resource allocation effect that resulted from the change. A change of mix that would have helpful macroeconomic effects may often have *some* adverse effects on the allocation of resources; though there may also be cases where there would be no costs – a 'free lunch', as it has been called – or even a net gain. But it is important to realise that those extreme cases (a 'free lunch') are not the only ones where a change towards a less inflationary mix is justified.

For rational economic policy-making involves assessing the relative advantages of alternative mixes from a macroeconomic point of view, and then also making judgments about the extent and direction of any resource allocation effects that a change of mix may have. It is not rational to adopt the widespread practice of failing to compare alternative macroeconomic mixes on the basis of their respective contributions to holding down the price level at any given level of employment; nor is it defensible to make the assumption that adverse resource allocation effects will generally result from a change to a less inflationary mix. Both the macroeconomic consequences and resource allocation effects have to be weighed before final decisions can rationally be taken.

Within this broader framework for deciding macroeconomic policy, however, the macroeconomic evidence discussed in earlier chapters is clearly consistent with the view that during recent periods when countries have been suffering from stagflation the settings of tax rates, government outlays and monetary policy have generally been changing in directions that *a priori* analysis suggests would have made it harder to hold down inflation at any given level of unemployment. If such problems are to be avoided in future, it is essential that macroeconomic policy decisions should take full account of this evidence, alongside the strong *a priori* grounds for believing that a very different macroeconomic mix from that generally applied between the later 1960s and the early 1980s must be used if stagflation is to be avoided in future.

Appendix: Testing the Macroeconomic Mix in the Major Seven OECD Countries*

TRAN VAN HOA

This Appendix outlines certain econometric tests designed to test the basic contentions of the present book. These are as follows:

1. that a rise in the ratio of taxes and other government current receipts to GDP tends to make it harder to hold down the price level in the immediately succeeding years;
2. that a rise in the ratio of total government outlays (or government transfer payments alone) makes it harder to hold down the price level in immediately succeeding years; and
3. that a relatively easy setting of monetary policy (as indicated by a relatively rapid monetary growth or a fall in real interest rates) tends to make it harder to hold down the price level in immediately succeeding years.

The intention is thus to test this partial explanation of inflation – as indicated by the rate of increase in the consumer price indexes (CPI) of the countries included in the tests. There is no attempt to provide a full explanation for inflation, and there is in fact a substantial residual element (a 'time trend') in the results which implies that many other influences were at work that were influencing the rise in the CPI. But explicit account is taken of one of these influences, namely, the fluctuations in the real price of oil; and that in fact turned out to have a significant association with the rise in the CPI.

The object of the tests was to see whether there was, on the average over the years covered, a significant relationship between the extent of the rise in the CPI in a particular year and the changes in the

*The author is indebted to Duncan Ironmonger for helpful suggestions in the preparation of this Appendix.

settings of each of these macroeconomic instruments over the immediately preceding two years.

The period covered was from 1967 to 1982, and data used were the changes from year to year in the relevant indicators for each of the major seven OECD countries – the US, Japan, West Germany, France, Britain, Italy and Canada. An allowance was made for the extent to which the experience of each of these countries diverged from the average by the inclusion of a 'dummy variable' for six of the seven countries; but the conclusions represent an average for the group as a whole (and should therefore not be interpreted as necessarily indicating the extent of the relationships in question for individual countries). The reason for including each country as a separate case is that the number of observations on which the tests were based was then naturally far greater than if an average for the group had been the basis for the conclusions.

The tests were designed to assess the relative importance (the relative weights) of the changes in the setting of the macro policy instruments in *each* of the two preceding years, as well as the strength (the coefficient) and direction (the sign – positive or negative) of the association between those changes and the rise in the CPI.

For the results to be consistent with the hypotheses outlined in the present book it would be necessary for there to be a significant and positive relationship between monetary growth in one or more of the immediately preceding years and the subsequent rise in the CPI; for relatively large rises in the 'tax ratio' (government current receipts to GDP) over a two-year period to be followed by a relatively large rise in the CPI; and for relatively large rises over the two preceding years in the ratio of government outlays (total, or transfers alone) to GDP to be followed by relatively sharp rises in the CPI. Note that it would have been consistent with the basic analysis of this book even if a tax rise had merely tended to be associated with a *lowering* of inflation – provided that its effect in reducing inflation was less than that of a reduction in government outlays having the same effect on employment or real output. It is therefore of special interest that the relationship between tax rises and inflation turned out, in fact, actually to be consistently positive (tax rises tending to be followed by *higher* inflation – with a given setting of the other instruments, including monetary growth).

The results showed that wherever there was a significant association between the indicators tested and the rise in the CPI, relatively large rises in either of the budgetary ratios tended to be followed by a relatively large increase in the CPI. For tax rates it was not always the change over the most recent year that had the largest and most significant apparent effect. This result is of special interest, because if it had been the rise in tax receipts in the most recent year that had been most clearly associated with a high rate of inflation one might have supposed that the relationship was mainly the result of inflation tending to cause the ratio of taxes to GDP to increase.

The relationship between the rise in the CPI and the increase in government outlays (especially in transfer payments alone) is also consistently positive; but in the case in which M2 was used as the monetary indicator it is the change in government outlays *in the most recent year* that has a greater weight and significance in the association than that of the earlier year.

For monetary growth we found that it was the change in the monetary growth rate two years previously (that is, *not* the change in the most recent year but in the previous one) that had a clear positive relationship with the rise in the CPI. We tested for other combinations of one or more of the three previous years and found that none of the other relationships of monetary growth with the rise in the CPI were statistically satisfactory as a whole. On the other hand, we found that an increase or decrease in the real rate of interest over the two preceding years had a significant (negative) relationship with the rise in the CPI. When the real rate of interest (as measured by the long-term bond rate adjusted by the rate of increase in the GDP deflator) falls, subsequent inflation clearly tends to be correspondingly greater.

We tested the results to see whether the inclusion of the level of unemployment as an additional explanatory variable showed unemployment as having a significant relationship with the rate of inflation as measured by the rise in the CPI; but found that the level of unemployment – though it clearly had a significant, (negative) relationship with inflation *when tested by itself* – turned out either to be *in*significant in its association with the rise in the CPI or to make the CPI equations unsatisfactory as a whole if included with the indicators of the policy mix. (This is clearly one of the most important results of the tests.) We also found that monetary growth alone was much less satisfactory as an explanation of inflation than any of the macro-mix equations.

It should be emphasised that tests such as these do not 'prove' a causative relationship. But if changes in the mix over the two preceding years had no bearing on the extent of inflation in a particular year it would be surprising to find results such as these; for they are clearly consistent with the view that the mix does matter – in the sense of influencing the extent of inflation as measured by the rise in the CPI in any given year. Furthermore, they are *not* consistent with the view that a high level of unemployment has a significant association with the extent of the rise in the CPI – apart from the mix of macroeconomic measures with which that level of unemployment is established. Taking these results together, therefore, the conclusions are consistent with the view that a high level of unemployment is not necessarily effective in reducing inflation; and that, even if it were, there are changes in the mix that would have a more consistent and predictable effect in holding down inflation than would a rise in unemployment.

READING THE RESULTS

The results show the coefficient for each of the indicators of the setting of the mix. For example, if the coefficient on the rise in the tax ratio were 0.2, this would mean that if there was an average annual rise of 1% in the tax ratio (say, from 30 to 30.3 in one year, or 30.3 to 30.6 over the next year), *and if each of those years had an equal weight*, one could expect inflation in the year under consideration to be 0.2 of a percentage point higher than it would otherwise have been (all else equal). But the results also show that the two years do not have exactly equal weights; they indicate the relative importance of each of the two years (adding up to 1) for the rise in the budgetary variables and the change in real interest rates. These relative weights have then to be applied to the change in the tax ratio (for example) in each of those two years, and then multiplied by the coefficient of tax rates on inflation to obtain a conclusion about the (weighted) average apparent effect of tax increases on the CPI.

For the monetary growth rates it turned out that only the change in the rate of monetary growth one year previously (that is, *not* the most recent year-to-year change, but only the year-to-year change over the preceding year) had a significant relationship with the rise in the CPI. The rise in the real price of oil in a given year had a consistent and significant relationship with the rise in the CPI *in the same year*.

We tested various combinations of changes in government total outlays or transfer payments alone and with monetary growth rates adjusted for the simultaneous rise in real GDP (that is, monetary growth per unit of GDP), as well as the unadjusted data, and also with the change in real interest rates. The results reported are the econometrically preferred combinations of changes in the macroeconomic instruments in that they turn out to have the most consistently significant relationships with the rate of increase in the CPI. But it is worth recording that on all the tests – in all of which the data were allowed to determine not only the coefficients but also the most significant weighting pattern for the variables – the signs on the budgetary variables were positive in all cases (whether or not they were statistically significant on the basis of the usual criteria). This seems a remarkably consistent ('robust') result to have found across a fairly wide range of different combinations of indicators of the policy mix.

As has been mentioned earlier, the framework we use for the analysis below is partial in the sense that only fiscal and monetary policy indicators are considered. In spite of this, the tests show the importance of the simultaneous and differential effects on inflation of a tax cut, an increase in government outlays or transfer payments, and money supply or interest rates.

The following paragraphs set out the nature and results of our tests in fuller and more technical detail.

1 THE DATA

The data in our analysis are annual data covering the period 1967 to 1982 for seven major OECD countries. These major OECD countries are the United States, Japan, West Germany, France, Britain, Italy and Canada. The data in all cases are compiled from the OECD *Economic Outlook* and *Historical Statistics*, supplemented, for more recent observations, by OECD *Main Economic Indicators*, and for monetary data the IMF's *International Financial Statistics*.

The data set consists of eight statistical series, all of which are coded in mnemonics for ease of reference. These series are:

CR : the percentage rate of change of the consumer price index.
M2 : the percentage ràte of change of M1 plus quasi-money (as defined by the IMF) at current prices and exchange rates.
LAR : the percentage rate of change of the ratio of total government outlays to GDP (e.g. the ratio moving from 30% to 33% is a 10% rate of change).
TRR : the percentage rate of change of the ratio of current government receipts to GDP.

PAR : the percentage rate of change of the ratio of government transfer payments to GDP. Transfer payments are defined as the difference between total current disbursements and final consumption expenditure by government.

U : the level of unemployment as a percentage of the total labour force, as standardised by the OECD.

RLR : the percentage point change in the real long-term rate of interest from the preceeding year (e.g. if the real long-term rate of interest is 15% in 1981 and 12% in 1980, RLR for 1981 is thus 3%). The real long-term rate of interest is the nominal long-term rate of interest divided by the GDP implicit price index.

ROR : the percentage rate of change of the weighted official/contract price of crude oil exports (fob), deflated by the rate of change of consumer prices (CR).

2 LINEAR CAUSAL RELATIONSHIPS

It should be noted that the specification of a price equation as indicated above assumes a causal relationship from the fiscal and monetary indicators or arguments to prices. This definition of causality is distinct from the statistical concept of causality. One way of testing for causation is the use of cross-spectral methods of the time-series analysis as proposed by Granger (1969) and others (see Pierce and Haugh (1977)). An earlier application of these methods to macroeconomic hypotheses was reported by Fels and Tran Van Hoa (1981) in an analysis of wage behaviour in Australia and by Tran Van Hoa (1981) in a study of wage and price movements in West Germany. Thus, in principle, it would be valid to test the macro-mix hypothesis by use of cross-spectral methods. In fact, a recent attempt at applying these methods to the macro-economic policy mix was reported by Stephens (1984) using United States data.

If testing for causation is required, a multidimensional cross-spectral approach (reflecting the various fiscal and monetary indicators) is more appropriate to our macro-mix model discussed earlier. In our case the cross-spectral method would involve the specification of a linear autoregressive-distributed lag (AD) model for CR and the determination of the existence or otherwise of the specific relationship would depend essentially on the inequality of forecast variances (or, equivalently, the likelihood ratio statistics). For quarterly models, a uniform lag structure of order four has usually been assumed by previous investigators for non-monetary variables. For annual models, the equivalent lag structure is thus of order one for non-monetary variables. Money in all its guises usually has a lag structure of order eight for quarterly models and thus of order two for annual data (see Sims (1972)).

As is also well-known (see Pierce and Haugh (1977)), the accuracy of the method of detection of causality depends essentially on the completeness of the information universe of the model under study. Strictly speaking, this requirement is not satisfied in our case where we make a partial analysis of the price behaviour. This analysis deals specifically with the effectiveness of fiscal and monetary policy variables in the explanation and control of consumer prices. Furthermore, a full formulation of the AD causal model for CR is severely restricted by the small sampling size of our annual data. In view of this, and also because prior information is often neglected in a causal model, except in the case of lag truncation, we are concerned below with a dynamic specification and efficient estimation of the CR equation in which specifically selected fiscal and monetary indicators are possible causes. In this sense, our model is of a class of limited information and with compressed dynamics. These novel modelling features will be explained more fully below.

3 NONLINEAR DYNAMIC SPECIFICATIONS

In spite of its simplicity, a first-order AD causal model of CR with one single explanatory variable must always encompass precisely nine typological representations of the linear data-generating process of CR (see Hendry, Pagan and Sargan (1983)). These nine subsets describe different lag structures and long-run responses of CR to its argument and can be used to discriminate among alternative specifications and generalisations (for an earlier application of this methodology in aggregate consumption analysis, see Tran Van Hoa (1983)). It should be noted, however, that this first-order AD causal model may not be adequate in describing macroeconomic behaviour. One particular example is the monetary effects on inflation, in which a second-order AD representation would be more consistent with extensive past experience. This necessitates the development of a more general and, in our view, more appropriate approach to modelling and testing the macro-mix hypothesis discussed in the text of the book. This new approach is described below and it can be regarded as a natural generalisation of the linear causal methodology and the conventional lag techniques.

Formally, a general linear AD formulation of the CR equation incorporating both fiscal and monetary instrument variables (i.e. TRR, LAR or PAR, M2 or RLR) with a uniform lag structure of order m can be written in full as:

$$\begin{aligned} \mathrm{CR}_t = \alpha_0 &+ \sum_{i=1}^{m} \alpha_{Ci}\mathrm{CR}_{t-i} + \sum_{i=0}^{m} \alpha_{Ti}\mathrm{TRR}_{t-i} + \sum_{i=0}^{m} \alpha_{Li}\mathrm{LAR}_{t-i} \\ &+ \sum_{i=0}^{m} \alpha_{Mi}M2_{t-i} + \sum_{i=0}^{m} \alpha_{Ui}U_{t-i} \\ &+ \sum_{i=0}^{m} \alpha_{Ri}\mathrm{ROR}_{t-i} + \alpha T_t + u_{ct}, \end{aligned} \tag{1}$$

where, in addition to the intercept, $\alpha_{\cdot i}$, (i = C, T, etc.) are the impact or distributed lag parameters, T_t a time trend and u_{ct} the disturbances with whitenoise or autocorrelation properties. It is clear that, written in this dynamic form, the CR equation satisfies the testing representations of linear causation in the sense of Wiener-Granger. In fact, when the disturbances are whitenoises, a linear summation of the lagged coefficients in each summand determines the presence (or absence) of an apparent causal relationship between our policy variables and the change in the CPI (see Fels and Tran Van Hoa, (1981)). This method is not used below for the reasons indicated in Section 2 above.

Consider now the nonlinear dynamic AD representation of CR given above. (The same notation for the parameters is used for convenience)

$$\begin{aligned} \mathrm{CR}_t = \alpha_0 &+ \alpha_C\overline{\mathrm{CR}_t} + \alpha_T\overline{\mathrm{TRR}_t} + \alpha_L\overline{\mathrm{LAR}_t} \\ &+ \alpha_M\overline{M2_t} + \alpha_U U_t \\ &+ \alpha_R\overline{\mathrm{ROR}_t} + \alpha T_t + u_{ct} \end{aligned} \tag{2}$$

where α_i are the combined effect parameters and the barred variables are compressed variables satisfying the relations

$$\overline{\mathrm{CR}_t} = \sum_{i=1}^{m} \alpha_{Ci}\mathrm{CR}_{t-i} \text{ with } \sum_{i=1}^{m} \alpha_{Ci} = 1 \quad (3)$$

$$\overline{\mathrm{TRR}_t} = \sum_{i=0}^{m} \alpha_{Ti}\mathrm{TRR}_{t-i} \text{ with } \sum_{i=0}^{m} \alpha_{Ti} = 1 \quad (4)$$

etc.

Formulated in this way, the CR equation (2) contains both estimable generalised rational distributed lags (3) and (4) etc. (see Maddala (1977)) and Wiener-Granger causation in an integrated filtering structure. In this structure, the effects of fiscal, monetary and other economic indicators are nonlinear or compounded and the lags follow no permanently decaying geometric pattern, but rather a finite-component distribution with generalised stochastic properties. From (2), if all effect parameters are set to unity, our integrated model of inflation reduces to the traditional distributed lag model in the Jorgenson sense. If all effect parameters are set to unity and no distributed lag coefficients are imposed *a priori*, our model then reduces to the familiar causal model in the Wiener-Granger sense. In this respect, both the Jorgenson and Wiener-Granger models can be regarded as subsets of the integrated model.

Obviously, given sufficient degrees of freedom, the equation (2) can be conveniently estimated by any standard nonlinear econometric estimation package. Furthermore, there is no reason why the order of the lags (that is, m) cannot be different for different explanatory variables. In theory then, estimates by scanning or grid search over the m range from (2), such as we give below, can be regarded as maximum likelihood estimates having desirable statistical properties. This is one important feature of our method.

Because we are using annual data in percentage form in our study, a lag structure of order two (a discussion of longer lags is given in section 4) has been specified for the equation (2). Within this lag structure, various hypotheses concerning the effects of fiscal, monetary and exogenous variables on inflation (CR) can be tested. In addition, some *a priori* or experiential information on the lag structure can be utilised.

First, the most obvious information is the limitation of the lag order as dictated by the size of sample data. The second kind of information is related to the delayed adjustment process which would indicate that the effects of the monetary aggregate M2 on inflation are unlikely to be instantaneous and probably follow a two-year lag as previous studies have indicated. The third kind of important information is concerned with the objective of our present study: that is, the significance or otherwise of the macro-policy mix in empirical studies. In other words, we wish to highlight the fiscal and monetary effects in the inflation equation and not merely to be involved in a forecasting exercise in which fiscal and monetary effects could be assumed to be imbedded in lagged movements of inflation. In this case, we therefore assume below that all autoregressive effects of inflation are zero or negligible. When autoregressiveness is omitted from the CR equation, our specification is in fact a generalisation of Fisherian or Almon lags and Weiner-Granger causation models.

The above discussion indicates that our estimated effect coefficients (α_T, α_L, etc.) and the lagged weighting patterns (α_{Ti}, α_{Li}, etc.) reported below are a mixture of pure data-based information (that is, the application of time-series AD analysis to data) and adaptive decision rules, in which economic-theoretic arguments and experimental evidence are used as *a priori* information in the flexible nonlinear dynamic specification (2) of inflation. Earlier uses of moving averages or filtered data (which are equivalent to distributed lagged data) to measure inflation variability and uncertainty include the work by Gupta (1982) and Khan and Abbas (1983) in their analysis of aggregate consumption and inflation in Latin American and Asian countries. The effect coefficients can be regarded as long-run coefficients in the sense of partial adjustment processes. In this context, the lagged weighting coefficients represent short-run adjustments.

In Tables A1 and A2, we report the principal findings of the various versions of the price equation fitted to data of the seven OECD countries mentioned earlier for the period 1967 to 1982. Each equation is of the seemingly unrelated form with augmented explanatory variables, seven country constants, and a linear time trend. As the dependent variable is identical in all versions of the CR equation, the application of a discriminatory test (such as the log likelihood ratio, the forecast variance inequality, and the explained sum of squared residuals) can be made so as to select statistically optimal equations. In the final equations, all parameter estimates conform to our theoretical expectations on their direction (sign) of influence, satisfy the significance conditions at the conventional critical level and appear economically plausible. The equations reported in Tables A1 and A2 are optimal alternative mixed dynamic price equations which, according to our criteria indicated above, can be discriminated with one another or with other price equations representing competing hypotheses.

4 SOME RESULTS

Tables A1 and A2 show for different instrument variables the effects of fiscal (that is, TRR and LAR or TRR and PAR) and monetary (that is, M2 or RLR) policy on the inflation rates of the seven main OECD countries, and all effect and distributed lag coefficients for these policy variables are reported. As can be seen from the tables, the lag structure of some of the economic indicators has been truncated to the second order or less. This was decided because the results of our analysis of the macro-mix model using three or four years in the lag structure appeared to be statistically less satisfactory.

From Tables A1 and A2, we note the following results:

1. Changes in the taxation ratio (TRR), the government transfer payments ratio (PAR), the government outlay ratio (LAR), and monetary growth (M2) all have a significant and positive association with the inflation rates, whilst changes in the real long-term rate of interest (RLR) have a strong negative association with inflation.
2. In both tables, a rise in the ratio of government current receipts to GDP averaging 1% over the two years tends to be associated with a subsequent rise of about 0.30 percentage points in consumer prices. The current year's rise in government receipts appears to be less important in affecting inflation rates than the previous year's when M2 is used as an indicator of monetary policy, but the opposite weighting pattern is observed when RLR is employed instead.
3. A rise in total government outlays as a ratio of GDP averaging one per cent over the two years tends to be associated with a rise of about 0.25 percentage points in consumer prices in the subsequent year. Approximately half of the weight is to be attributed to the rise in total government outlays in each of the two years, with slightly more weight attributable to the most recent year when M2 is employed.
4. A rise in the monetary aggregate M2 of 1% tends to be associated with a rise of 0.26% in consumer prices a year later.

Current inflation rates appear unaffected by current changes in M2.

5. A fall in the real long-term rate of interest averaging 1% over two years tends to be associated with a rise of about 0.70% in consumer prices in the following year, with each of the two years being of approximately equal importance.
6. The real price of oil (ROR) and the time trend (T) both have significant and positive effects on inflation rates. Furthermore, these effects are instantaneous and contain negligible lagged adjustments.

5 THE MACRO-MIX AND COMPETING HYPOTHESES

The empirical findings reported above appear to lend statistical support to the hypothesis of macro-mix policy. Although the results are derived from the data set of only seven major OECD countries for the period 1967 to 1982, these results satisfy conventional statistical tests of significance of individual parameter estimates and are thus acceptable in the econometric sense. In fact, similar results were obtained when the data set was truncated to the period 1967 to 1981 only.

The robustness of the empirical findings reported can be further analysed within the given data set by means of tests of alternative hypotheses in relation to policy to control inflation. The two competing hypotheses we consider for a comparative study below are (a) the effects of unemployment on inflation and (b) the single-instrument macro policy of the monetary aggregate M2. As some of the competing hypotheses are non-nested (see below), the likelihood ratio is an appropriate criterion to be adopted for the testing procedure. In large samples this statistic is consistent and unbiased and has a chi-squared distribution with the degrees of freedom equal to the number of restrictions imposed on the parameters when the null hypothesis is true. Furthermore, most of the other tests commonly use in statistics and econometrics can be derived from the likelihood ratio method (Maddala (1977)).

In Tables A3 and A4, we present the likelihood ratio statistics and their degrees of freedom to evaluate the dominance of each of the four integrated macro-mix equations as reported in Tables A1 and A2 (these equations hereafter being called the pure macro-mix equations) and each of the relevant competing hypotheses. In addition to the inclusion of real oil prices, a linear time trend and seven country constants, these competing hypotheses are also formulated in the nonlinear dynamic form used for the pure macro-mix equations and comprise:

Single-instrument policy

Hypothesis 1: The monetary aggregate M2 as the sole policy influence in the inflation (CR) equation.

Hypothesis 2: The level of unemployment as the sole influence in the inflation (CR) equation.

Augmented macro-mix policy

Hypothesis 3: The inclusion of unemployment in the pure macro-mix (CR) equation containing TRR, LAR, and M2.

Hypothesis 4: The inclusion of unemployment in the pure macro-mix (CR) equation containing TRR, LAR, and RLR.

Hypothesis 5: The inclusion of unemployment in the pure macro-mix (CR) equation containing TRR, PAR, and M2.

Hypothesis 6: The inclusion of unemployment in the pure macro-mix (CR) equation containing TRR, PAR, and RLR.

The equations representing Hypotheses 3-6 are called for convenience the augmented macro-mix equations.

From Tables A3 and A4, the following results are obtained:

1. Statistically, the evidence reported is not strong enough to discriminate significantly between the pure and the augmented macro-mix equations. In other words, nothing is gained – and, in fact, some loss of significance is sustained – by introducing unemployment as an additional policy variable in the pure macro-mix equations presented above. This is true regardless of which monetary policy variable (that is, M2 or the real long-term rate of interest, RLR) and which fiscal policy variables (that is, TRR and LAR, or TRR and PAR) are employed. In this context, the pure macro-mix equations are statistically and economically optimal.

2. On the other hand, all of the pure macro-mix equations are superior to the inflation equations that use either M2 or unemployment alone as the single control on inflation. This evidence seems to confirm the dominance of the macro-mix hypothesis over other single-instrument policy hypotheses for the present set of international time-series data.

TABLE A.1 *Effects on inflation rates*

	(I)		(II)	
Fiscal policy variables	TRR	LAR	TRR	PAR
Effect Coefficient	0.296(1.84)	0.221(1.74)	0.331(2.15)	0.188(2.06)
Lag 0:t	0.414(1.37)	0.553(2.06)	0.406(1.52)	0.571(2.51)
Lag 1:t–1	0.586	0.447	0.594	0.429
Monetary policy variables	M2		M2	
Effect Coefficient	0.266(3.48)		0.260(3.44)	
Lag 0:t	0.000		0.000	
Lag 1:t–1	1.000		1.000	
Other variables	OIL	TIME	OIL	TIME
Effect Coefficient	0.021(3.38)	0.413(4.89)	0.022(3.37)	0.403(4.80)
Country constants				
United States	1.158		1.216	
Japan	−1.290		−1.565	
Germany	−1.780		−1.580	
France	1.933		2.061	
Britain	4.689		4.779	
Italy	3.918		4.036	
Canada	−3.264		−3.353	
Summary statistics				
LF	–243.608		–242.832	
R2	0.629		0.635	
N	97		97	

Notes LF: Log of likelihood function.
R2: Explained sum of squared residuals.
N: Number of observations.
Estimated t-statistic in parentheses.

TABLE A2 *Effects on inflation rates*

	(III)		(IV)	
Fiscal policy variables	TRR	LAR	TRR	PAR
Effect Coefficient	0.294(1.81)	0.297(2.28)	0.330(2.13)	0.266(2.89)
Lag 0:t	0.591(1.92)	0.473(2.27)	0.562(2.13)	0.465(2.90)
Lag 1:t–1	0.409	0.527	0.438	0.535
Monetary policy variables	RLR		RLR	
Effect Coefficient	−0.671(3.25)		−0.702(3.46)	
Lag 0:t	0.473(4.02)		0.467(4.30)	
Lag 1:t–1	0.527		0.533	
Other variables	OIL	TIME	OIL	TIME
Effect Coefficient	0.020(2.97)	0.503(5.55)	0.020(2.99)	0.498(5.56)
Country constants				
United States	0.140		−0.267	
Japan	−1.236		−1.659	
Germany	−3.122		−2.837	
France	1.732		1.891	
Britain	4.451		4.555	
Italy	4.553		4.650	
Canada	−0.839		−1.170	
Summary statistics				
LF	−244.352		−242.647	
R2	0.623		0.636	
N	97		97	

TABLE A3 *Macro-mix and competing hypotheses: Likelihood ratio statistics*

	Hypo 1 *M2*	*Hypo 2* *U*	*Hypo 3* *TRR,LAR,M2,U*	*Hypo 4* *TRR,LAR,RLR,U*	*Hypo 5* *TRR,PAR,M2,U*	*Hypo 6* *TRR,PAR,RLR,U*
TRR,LAR,M2	10.8**	17.2**	5.4*	–	–	–
TRR,LAR,RLR	12.9**	15.7**	–	1.5*	–	–
TRR,PAR,M2	12.3**	18.7**	–	–	4.2*	–
TRR,PAR,RLR	16.3**	19.1**	–	–	–	1.9*

Notes * Not significant at the 5% critical level

** Significant at the 5% critical level

Hypo 1–6: Hypotheses 1 to 6 as discussed in the text.

The coordinate of the labels defines the pair of competing hypotheses being tested for possible dominance or difference.

This table shows that the pure macro-mix hypotheses in the left hand column are significantly superior to the single-instrument policy of M2 or U taken alone. The table shows that the addition to the pure macro-mix of unemployment does not significantly improve the statistical explanation of inflation.

TABLE A4 *Macro-mix and competing hypotheses: Degrees of freedom*

Equation		*Hypo 1* *M2*	*Hypo 2* *U*	*Hypo 3* *TRR,LAR,M2,U*	*Hypo 4* *TRR,LAR,RLR,U*	*Hypo 5* *TRR,PAR,M2,U*	*Hypo 6* *TRR,PAR,RLR,U*
	K	*10*	*11*	*16*	*17*	*16*	*17*
TRR,LAR,M2	14	4	3	2	–	–	–
TRR,LAR,RLR	15	5	4	–	2	–	–
TRR,PAR,M2	14	4	3	–	–	2	–
TRR,PAR,RLR	15	5	4	–	–	–	2

Notes K: The number of parameters in the equation.
The critical significances at the 5% level for the likelihood ratio statistics for different degrees of freedom (df) are: 1df, 3.84; 2df, 5.99; 3df, 7.81; 4df, 9.49 and 5df, 11.10.

Bibliography

Note: This bibliography includes only works referred to in the text or works published since the compilation of the earlier bibliographies in *The Macroeconomic Mix to Stop Stagflation* and *Unemployment, Inflation and New Macroeconomic Policies*.

Argy, V. (1981), *The Postwar International Money Crisis – an Analysis*, London, Allen & Unwin.

Dernberg, T. F. (1974), 'The Macroeconomic Implications of Wage Retaliation Against Higher Taxation', *International Monetary Fund Staff Papers*.

Fels, A. and Tran Van Hoa (1981), 'Causal Relationships in Australian Wage Inflation and Minimum Award Rates', *Economic Record*.

Granger, C. W. T. (1969), 'Investigating Causal Relationships by Econometric Models and Cross Spectral Methods', *Econometrica*.

Gupta, K. L. (1982), 'Inflation, Its Viability and Consumption in Selected Latin American Countries', *Economics Letters*.

Hendry, E. I., Pagan, A. R. and Sargan, J. D. (1983), 'Dynamic Specification' in Griliches, Z. and Intriligator, M. D. (eds), *Handbook of Econometrics*, Amsterdam, North Holland Co., forthcoming.

Khan, A. H. and Abbas, K. (1983), 'Additional Evidence on Inflation Variability: The Experience of Asian Countries', *Economics Letters*.

Jones, R. S. and Perkins, J. O. N. (1981), *Contemporary Macroeconomics*, Sydney, Prentice-Hall (2nd edition, forthcoming 1985).

Maddala, G. S. (1977), *Econometrics*, New York, McGraw-Hill.

McDonald, I.M., 'Anti-Stagflationary Tax Cuts and the Problem of Investment', *Economic Record* (1986).

Meade, J. E., Vines, David and Maciejowski, J. M., (1982) *Stagflation*, vol. 1 Wage-fixing and (1982) vol. 2, *Demand Management*, Allen & Unwin.

Perkins, J. O. N. (1979), *The Macroeconomic Mix to Stop Stagflation*, London, Macmillan.

Perkins, J. O. N. (1982), *Unemployment, Inflation and New Macroeconomic Policy*, London, Macmillan.

Pierce, D. A. and Haugh, L. D. (1977), "Causality in Temporal Systems: Characterizations and a Survey", *Journal of Econometrics*.

Sachs, J. D. 'Real Wage Rates and Unemployment in OECD countries', *Brookings Papers in Economic Activity*, 1, 1983.

Sims, C. A. (1972), 'Money, Income and Causality', *American Economic Review*.

Smyth, D. J. (1982), 'Income taxes, Labour Supply, Output and the Price Level', *Public Finance*, XXXVII, 1.

Stephens, J. Kirker (1980), 'Inflation, Unemployment and the Macroeconomic Policy Mix', Center for Economic and Management Research, University of Oklahoma, 1980.

Stephens, J. Kirker (1984), 'Some Tentative Results on Causality and the Macroeconomic Policy Mix', paper presented to the Midsouth Academy of Economists.

Tran Van Hoa (1981), 'Causality and Wage Price Inflation in West Germany: 1964 to 1979', *Weltwirtschaftliches Archiv* (Review of World Economics).

Tran Van Hoa (1983), 'An All-encompassing Consumption Function: the Australian Case', *Economics Letters*.

Index